Soul Shaker

A Whirlwind Awakening

My Naked Truth of Resilience
Beyond the Scar

Catherine Kontos

Be the seed that plants its roots
and flourishes when life seems impossible.

– C. Kontos

Soul Shaker/A Whirlwind Awakening
My Naked Truth of Resilience Beyond the Scar

Canadian Intellectual Property Office | An Agency of Industry Canada

Soul Shaker
Copyright Registration No.: 1153220 © 2018
© 2018 Catherine Kontos
www.catherinekontos.com

ISBN: 978-1-68757447-3

Disclaimer
This book contains the ideas and opinions of its author. The book intends to provide information, helpful content, and motivation to readers. It is shared and sold with the understanding that the author is not engaged to render psychological, medical, legal, or any other personal or professional advice. No warranties or guarantees are expressed or implied by the author's choice to include any of the content in this volume. Readers should consult their medical or accredited health providers before adopting any of the suggestions in this book or drawing any ideas, inferences or practices from this book. The author shall not be liable for any physical, psychological, emotional, financial, or commercial damages, including – but not limited to – special, incidental, consequential, or other damages. Readers are responsible for their own choices, actions and results.

1st Edition, 1st Printing 2019
Cover Design Creative Director: Catherine Kontos
Cover Design: Steve Walters at Carolyn Flower International
– www.carolynflower.com
Interior Design: Steve Walters
Cover Photo: Wanda Malfara
Interior Painting Illustration: Catherine Kontos
Author Photo: Wanda Malfara

Table of Contents

i DEDICATION

In memory of my cherished cousin – my mentor bearing the same name as me, Catherine Kontos – who passed away from leukemia in 2012.

You were very present in my heart and mind during my journey. Little could I have known how your words during your battle would be the foundation and motivation to help me when no others could. I thank you for preparing me for battle by showing such fierceness during your two-year fight.

And to all the brave men, women and children battling cancer and its after-effects; to anyone who has suffered loss and has contemplated giving up on their dreams, or even their life; to all those who have been hurt by the hand of others; your stories are your legacy. They give strength to others.

Feel it.

Taste it.

Grasp it.

Continue being brave with your life.

Stop surviving. Start thriving.

ii INTRODUCTION

You gain strength, courage, and confidence by every experience in which you really stop to look fear in the face. You are able to say to yourself, "I lived through this horror. I can take the next thing that comes along."

– Eleanor Roosevelt

J ust because we're molded one way doesn't mean we can't break the mold and reshape ourselves.

Being human means there are times when we're faced with situations that we think we cannot bear. We get nervous and do whatever we can to avoid having to deal; maybe we slip things under the rug or keep ourselves so busy thinking "it" will go away. But then, there are times when what scares us most is also the thing that forces us to face the fear.

I had been struggling with a failing business and a troubled marriage and I kept myself over-busy, pretending everything was okay. As long as I was socializing, active and achieving, I believed everything would fall into place, but instead of things working out, I got the biggest scare of my life. I was diagnosed with an aggressive cancer. In the paralyzing moment of hearing that news, all the stresses, anxieties and fears that consumed my life before disappeared. That's when *Fear* and I met close up and I knew that the way I was managing my life had to change. I knew that there were only two choices: give in to the justifiable fear that I could die, or stare fear in the face and fight.

Time stopped, but I had to go on. This book is about how I cleaned up messes in my life, even as I was battling cancer. No matter what your battles, all that matters is that you find the courage to examine yourself and make it to the other side of fear because that's where your best life lies.

The moment I made the decision to fight, an apocalyptic shift happened within me. I felt the shaking of my soul, and when that passed, I was already changed. In seconds, I relinquished my attachment to fear. Serenity washed over me, and I grew calm, the calmest I had ever been in my life. This was the beginning of my awakening; I believe this can happen only when we break from what we believe is us and re-emerge into a new and different self. Free from past burdens and opening us to receive the lessons from those burdens. It's all about shifting perspective; the soul needs to be shaken to get there; hopefully you build the resilience to withstand the break.

Everything we go through has the power to either break us or build us. I decided nothing I was going through would break me. I became resilient and kept building on that resiliency through faith.

Have faith, build faith, and always remember that bravery isn't being unafraid; it's being afraid and doing something anyway.

All of this provided me with the inner space to put faith ahead of fear and finally confront the pain; failures and falls; losses and divorce; sickness, diagnosis, and treatment. The key was in trusting the journey and having the faith that all would work out.

Having faith gets us there. Building resilience gets us up after every blow. Together, they transform a life guided by fear into a life we love. And one of the best, most unlikely ways to get there is gratitude.

Gratitude?

When it seems as if everything that could go wrong is going wrong... gratitude?

But this always happens to me.

Why me???

You see those questions are your automatic, conditioned response to a bad situation. Nobody jumps for joy saying,

"Yessssss! I'm sick!"

"Woohoo! I've got cancer!"

......Silence. You cringe.

It's unsettling to hear those words and they bring with them an instantaneous discomfort. What if they were true? If true, life would be indelibly changed. And with that, the mind is flooded with a string of questions and self-blame... relentless, repeated torment.

Why me??

Why the hell me?????

It's a mistake.

What did I do?

Where did I go wrong?

It's my fault...

I should have. I could have...

I'm being punished.

All these thoughts came to me faster than a Porsche 911 speeding on a racetrack. It was in a matter of seconds when the doctor was looking down at his paper, refraining from looking up at me, that he spoke the words that would shake my soul, life as I knew it, right to the core of its existence.

It was in that fraction of time that my earthquake became both my complete collapse and my rebirth, giving rise to my awakening.

As we learn to have faith in the journey, we acquire peace in our soul and freedom for our mind to just be.

– Catherine Kontos

iii ENDORSEMENTS

"This is a bold and brave book. It's one all women – and men – must read and learn from. Catherine Kontos' candid account of her battle with cancer, the collapse of her marriage and the work it took to reinvent herself as a single mother and entrepreneur is powerful and inspiring. What Catherine understands, and you should too, is that wellness is about more than health – it's about the community we build together."

– Julie Quenneville,
McGill University Health Centre Foundation President

"I have been a breast cancer surgeon for 35 years – from the moment a person is diagnosed with breast cancer to the end of her journey. And the journey is a life-changer. Catherine Kontos describes and explains her journey in detail, highlighting her ups and downs, fears and joys. This is an honest and inspiring book and a must-read for any patient with cancer. I plan to recommend it to my patients."

– Dr. Gordon Brabant, M.D.C.M., FRCS (C)

"A heartwarming read that leaves you wanting more. Catherine has captured in this book that life is precious, and no matter what challenges you go through it is very possible to live your life with purpose. A strong and inspirational woman, that not only captures our hearts with her story but reminds us, that you can live your best life every single day, even after a breast cancer diagnosis. She is an example of doing just that. Bravo Catherine!"

– Denise Vourtzoumis,
Pink in the City Foundation – President

"Since I first met her in my early twenties, Catherine has embodied the characteristics of a pillar of strength: hope, genuineness, charisma and cheerfulness. She is a true friend, soul sister, and mentor. Her inspiring and soul-shaking book reminds me of the many challenges, obstacles, fears and victories she has lived through. Her book, *Soul Shaker*, imparts a powerful message, revealing the rollercoaster ride of heart-breaking challenges that she not only encountered head-on but survived with strength. Living life with an abundance of hope, living her dreams as she has never done before.

Soul Shaker will motivate you through your darkest moments, giving you hope and strength to overcome life's challenges with exhilarating energy going forward!!"

– Toni Coletti, Sanofi Pharmaceuticals,
Manager of Clinical Trials and Regulatory Affairs

"Catherine manifested how, after the battle has ended, you can choose to come out of it living an optimal life by practicing gratitude; as a result, experiencing a deep appreciation for life.

Soul Shaker is a powerful book that I would recommend to everybody who has been touched by cancer in one way or another.

Catherine Kontos might be a Resiliency coach, but she is first and foremost an extraordinary person."

– Louis Sanson, Breast Cancer Survivor,
Canada Border Services Agency / Government of Canada
– Intelligence Officer, Enforcement / Intelligence Division

"Catherine Kontos' book *Soul Shaker* is an anthem of survival through resiliency. Life lessons from a woman who met up with fear, summoned the courage to face it, found the gift in each collapse, and harnessed the power of will to overcome life's adversities. Catherine's recounting of her story is raw, real and honest. This book will meet you at the very places your fears have nested, and inspire you to transform them into triumphs. Truly Inspirational!"

– Taline Tarpinian,
True Bloom Coaching – Founder

Soul Shaker
A Whirlwind Awakening

My Naked Truth of Resilience
Beyond the Scar

Chapter One

The Breeding Ground
for *Dis-ease*

*A heart beats 115,000 times each day. Each beat, each throb,
each pulse sends you a message and it reads, "YOU'RE ALIVE!"...
you just need to listen TO COME ALIVE.*

– Catherine Kontos

You Wished it. You Got it.

I was 40 years old. I ate healthily, choosing fresh homemade organic foods; I exercised three times a week, like clockwork. I was, according to my GP, in optimum physical condition. My body mass index, my bloods, everything was on point. And, there was no family history of breast cancer. So how is it that a healthy, active, very-much-alive, 40-year-old woman comes face-to-face with everyone's most feared words?

"*YOU* have cancer."

It hit me like a freight train. I threw my arms up in the air, looked up, and said, "I give up." I thought I was doing things right, so it hit hard to realize that I had no control and that I had to let go my misconception of "control". No matter what I had done or would do, I couldn't predict outcomes. This was a hard thing to accept for a worrier. What a waste of time and energy it is to worry. I mean, worry about what? If I worry about it, does it mean it won't happen because I thought of it? How delusional is that? How does the fear of getting cancer prevent me from getting cancer?

At the time of my diagnosis, I had been working morning to night in a very stressful environment. Nothing seemed to be going right. Not at work and not at home. I was all over the place but going nowhere, running on fumes and circles. Nobody around me was happy. I felt it coming. All of it. One by one, everything I ever feared was inevitably going to happen. And this wasn't the familiar pangs of anxiety that I was accustomed to; no, this was an instinctual gut feeling of pending doom, unlike any I had ever had before.

I was a go-getter, waking in the morning, grabbing my coffee and running out the door. All day, every day; scratching to-do's off my list, often I would be eating only in the evening. I would simply forget to eat. I had no appetite, and I was losing weight. I would then come home and continue working in desperation and in hopes that I could get my business running. I felt alone in this battle. Completely alone and scared, but always believing that if I kept working hard, if I ran myself to the ground, it would pay off. Isn't that what everyone tells you?

"You have to work hard to play hard."

"Determination and perseverance pay off."

"Stay focused on your dream and you will achieve."

"Never give up…."

And so on. I was doing everything I could. Everything I knew and was told to do. Thinking to myself, *Maybe in a month, I'll get it done.* That month would come and go. Then I would think, *OK, perhaps this month.* That month came and went, as well. Nobody can take on the work of three people and get all of it done. I take responsibility for trusting blindly, so I can't blame anyone but me. The dream in my mind was so powerful that I thought it was foolproof. My mind was so focused on making it a reality that the excitement caused me to overlook some very important factors that eventually hurt my business and me as well.

I had a loan under my name and money invested; my reputation was now in jeopardy. This had to work, no matter what: failure was not an option. The pressure was intense. Everyone believed in me and my dream, and they were truly excited to see me make it happen. It had to work or I'd let everyone down. I couldn't let that happen. I wouldn't. Most of all, I would let myself down. The pressure was all on me.

> *Don't be so busy in life trying to make a dollar that you forget to live.*
>
> – **Catherine Kontos**

Something had to give; and sure enough finally did give. I felt myself starting to crack; my mind first, then my body. One day I came home sick inside and had to tell my family that I couldn't do it anymore. I went straight to my bedroom, shut the door and crawled into bed with the lights out. I lay over the covers, curled in the fetal position with my face buried in the pillow, sobbing uncontrollably. This had become my daily habit these days. But this time was different: the room felt darker and the air thicker. My chest hurt from all the crying; I could hardly breathe knowing that I had nothing to show for all my hard work and aware that this would be another blow to my marriage. I felt as though a demon was cornering me from all angles. I became so disillusioned and hopeless that all I could do was pray for the worst. And that's exactly what I did, without any further thought, I asked God to make me sick. Over and over again with conviction, I repeated out loud,

"Please God make me sick. Please I beg you… I want to die…"

It was my way out. Out of this failing business. Out of this marriage. Out of this life. Just out. This way I could at least say, "I am sick, I have to stop."

At least then I wouldn't be a failure. I fell asleep that night, crying and gasping into my tear-stained pillow.

Two days later, I rose from my bed, grabbed my coffee and left for work. As I headed north on the 75-kilometer drive to the Laurentian mountains north of Montreal on that cloud-covered day, my surroundings turned from spring to winter. Not only would the temperature drop cold, but so would my heart upon entering the empty Goliath of a building where I worked. I sat at the desk in my third-floor office staring out through big, white frame windows, far into the snow-covered lake and mountains. A place I used to fantasize about going to every morning was now dispiriting to me. Everything was dark: no glitter of light as I sat alone in this huge estate that was my business. I felt completely lost and alone.

Suddenly my face went numb on the left side; my eye started to twitch uncontrollably. I became anxious and fearful. I tried intentional, focused breathing to help me relax, but the twitching and numbness got worse: my arms, my legs, even my torso. I began to cry. What's going on? Then I remembered what I had asked for just two days prior. Was I getting my wish? This couldn't be. Little did I know the power that my mind and my words had over my body.

No, God, no. I thought.

As the minutes went by, the symptoms grew worse. I couldn't explain it, but they felt different from what I had experienced before. I grabbed my things and left for home. I had prayed to God for it, and God had given it to me: it was the beginning of my illness. As sure as I know my name, I knew this: Something in my body had changed that day, and I now believe that this was the day my DNA mutated and gave me cancer.

This was not my first time having these symptoms. Soon after I graduated from university, I had begun to suffer from symptoms of vertigo, migraines and daily pain. As time passed, they worsened to the point that I began to have extreme twitching and numbness. Doctors were convinced I was showing signs of multiple sclerosis, and so the testing had begun, but it all came back inconclusive. I was diagnosed with fibromyalgia and chronic migraines.

The pain from my headaches was paralyzing, and I had to cease work. After a year and a half of daily pain, I met a doctor at the pain clinic who was finally able to help me and steered me in the right direction to be cured, allowing me to take control of my health: no more processed foods. I started making my meals from scratch and drinking fresh vegetable juice a few times a day, working out three to four times a week; I started seeing a psychologist to help me deal better with my pain. A year later, with all my self-therapies, many of my symptoms had subsided, including the fibromyalgia. My doctor was so pleased that she used me as an example to all her team, as to how a patient can help themselves without the use of medication if they stick to a strict, disciplined regimen. It was a scary time, and it showed me how drastically life could change in a snap. Now, eight years later, it did again.

Chapter Two

The Hellfire Before
the Storm

With everyday hustle, we are inevitably overtaken by responsibilities.
Whether it's work, running around for our children, our daily chores…
how can we focus on ourselves and find balance? The mind's clutter
is too much, the body is tired, and decisions become hard to make.
We always seem to be running out of time.

– Catherine Kontos

Striving and Failing the Dream

I had waited a long time to fulfill my dream of owning my own business. A business where I could help others. I started pitching my ideas and speaking to potential partners before deciding to invest in a private luxury rehabilitation and therapy home for those suffering from addiction and nervous breakdowns. Eventually, I found the perfect lakeside property: everything seemed to be going my way. It was a building with bright yellow wood siding and many large windows overlooking the lake and mountains for miles on end. It was running as a bed and breakfast. So grand. So perfect. Yet so old and neglected. But I didn't care because my business plan was promising and the bank was backing me.

My business got a two-page spread in a very popular American magazine. I was ready to fly with it; so what if the building was old? I wholeheartedly loved this place and believed it was a sure thing, so I devoted every ounce of myself to make it so. The building would be maintained easily with the income it would generate. What could go wrong? Well, only EVERYTHING. One by one: my life, work, and health crumbled.

Depression is seeing only darkness in life with no hope for even a glitter of light. It's mourning that seems to never end. Too many are living in such a deep dark hole. Most give up trying to get help because they're so deep in their depression and have become completely hopeless. Please don't let that ever be you.

– Catherine Kontos

After six months of working seven days a week on my dream business, it was time to stop. The pain I felt and the sorrow deep in my heart were immeasurable. I was grieving the loss of a dream; all the money invested was lost, and I was so embarrassed by my failure. How would I face my family and tell them?

"I'm sorry, but I can't anymore."

Failure can be heart-wrenching. I had no choice. Little did I know that this was the beginning of what would be the darkest phase of my life.

As soon as I arrived home, I knew I needed to act fast to stop what was happening to my body. It had reached its limit. I went into a strategic mode and made decisions focused on what I needed to do to get better and stop whatever was happening to me.

I made phone calls. One was to my family. I told them what my body was experiencing and that I needed to get away. The next call was to my neurologist, asking him if I could get away and be prescribed a medication to alleviate the twitching and numbing. As soon as I got the okay, I called my travel agent telling her exactly which country and which hotel to book. By the time she called back to tell me I was booked, my bags had already been packed. I sent my colleagues a text to say that I'd be leaving the next day. At this point, I was a walking zombie. Pale, thin, lifeless. My cheeks were concave and my eyes dark; a shell of a person completely depleted of physical and emotional energy, depleted of spirit. The life had been sucked out of me. I was scared and broken

Running with Fear - Living for Others' Approval

Imagine waking up from a nightmare and the relief you feel when you realize it was just a bad dream. It was like that except I never woke up from the bad dream. My life had become a living nightmare. I went to sleep with a mind full of demons and woke up to demons chasing me, backing me into corners I could not escape. I was overcome with anxiety; not only was I broken, but everything I had built my life on was also broken, irreparably. The mental tyranny throughout those months was taking a toll on me. I felt like I had lost all control of my life.

When the core of your being is shaken, that's a sign that there's a gap between who you are acting as and who you really need to be. This gap exists because you've strayed more and more from who you are. Either because of societal pressures, life circumstances, or even shattered dreams. You may have given up or you probably just never noticed you were straying. Then one day you wake up and you don't even recognize yourself.

If you are not happy with your life, today is the day you need to stop living miserably and begin reviving the person you once were and become that person once again. Every minute passed is a minute lost. Stop wasting time and live the rest of your life with a smiling heart.

– Catherine Kontos

The next day, I took my 10-year-old daughter, Nikki, and we flew to Mexico for a five-day getaway. I was very tired and explained to her that I needed to relax and catch up on sleep so I could feel better. So every day we'd make our way to the pool area where I sat under the soothing sun while she played. We'd eat dinner at 7 p.m., and by 8 p.m. I was asleep. I don't even know how I managed to make it to 8 p.m.

While there, we went for mommy-daughter massages. Her excitement was contagious. She was the lifeline I grasped to gather my strength. Her smile and bright eyes injected me with the energy that I so desperately needed. As I lay on the massage table, she came running across the room naked, jumped on her table, whisked the covers over her and in a high-pitched perky voice said, "So, what do I do now?"

It was the sweetest gift to see her happy and so full of innocence. I chuckled and said, "You just lie down, sweetheart, and relax."

She plopped down, turned her head on the table and that was it. Silence.

That silence was priceless. There had been so much noise around me for so long that my mind and soul were suffocated by it. I could no longer think or process. It was torture living in my mind. Anyone who suffers from depression and anxiety understands what I mean. It's like you are in this cage with thoughts running through your mind and you know you need to get out, but you can't. And as these thoughts keep racing through your mind over and over again; you can't make them stop.

This is where the torture lies: you feel powerless like a caged bird, and the cage is your mind. How do you stop them? You try and try to feel better, but these thoughts overpower you. And then you think: *Better to end it all.* Because it's exhausting, the struggle of constantly feeling this mental pain seems pointless. This is where you need to really look deep in your soul and find the hope and courage to hold on until the storm in your mind passes, so you can get up, open that cage and release the bird to soar.

I always found this light in my daughter and in my faith. My daughter was my every reason to hang on, to believe that I was strong, and to have faith that I would not be defeated. Like a fighter in a ring, I thought: *They may have knocked me down, but I won't stay down. They will see me get up. At that last second when they think they have won, I rise strong to fight, to live.*

No one – absolutely no one – should ever allow to anyone to break their spirit. They can try, and they will, but I will be damned if I let them…and with those thoughts, I gathered enough strength to flap my clipped wings and learn to fly once again.

On the massage table with my most precious daughter next to me, far from everything and everyone, I felt peace wash over me for the first time in a long time. As the massage came to an end, the massage therapists walked away, telling us to ring the bell when we were ready to rise. After a few minutes, I heard the sound of a bell. I opened my eyes, and there was my precious angel, holding the bell, signaling my time to get up and be with her. She was my light now and my light always.

On Day 5 of our trip, although I still had symptoms, I felt stronger and more able to participate in some physical activity. I wanted to reward my daughter for being so helpful. So what else to do but go ziplining? I did say I wanted to let my caged bird fly, didn't I? So, Nikki and I flew. We flew through the mountains of the Mayan Riviera like birds. It was so liberating. I felt the wind on my face, through my hair, as I watched nature's beauty beneath me and said to myself, *This is how I want to live... This is freedom.*

The thing about my character was that no matter how hard I fell; I didn't stay down for long. I got up, I brushed off the dirt and continued. Resiliency is a necessity, not only in surviving the challenges but in propelling ourselves up from the bottom and thriving from the teachings that our failures teach us.

Resiliency is getting back up; again and again, no matter what. It's a state of mind. It's turning what is seemingly impossible into possible. It's refusing to allow sadness to overpower the will to live. No matter how low you're feeling, resiliency forces you out of the malaise. The opposite is true if you stay home and wallow in your sorrows. You go into a deeper state of sadness.

> *It's in that one moment you take to finally make that decision. This is where destiny is shaped.*
>
> **– Catherine Kontos**

Upon my return from Mexico, it was back to reality. And the reality was that the circumstances of my life were overwhelming my ability to think things through: I felt stuck, indecisive and dispirited. I urgently needed to wrap my head around where I was at and what I needed to do.

But first, a visit to my father's final resting place was in order. It was a sunny day. I lay a blue blanket on the grass by his headstone, where a tree provided me shadow from the sun's rays. I sobbed as I sat looking at his picture that adorned the stone. Tears poured down my face as I realized that I had become my dad.

He too had a business. His partner took advantage of his kindness, and at the age of 57, my dad went bankrupt, losing everything. But because he was a man of integrity, he had made sure that each one of his employees was paid after the doors closed. Even if it meant taking the shirt off his back to do so. He was the nicest man. Too nice at times.

I was only 15; too young to really understand what it meant to lose everything, but old enough to feel the pain, shame and guilt that my dad had felt. Old enough to see that it had broken him. Consumed with depression, he still needed to support us, so he woke up every morning, swallowed his pride and went to work for a man who was once his competitor. His new coworkers had been his previous employees. Imagine building a successful business, and as a result of two bad deals back-to-back, watching your business crumble into nothing.

Seeing my father lose it all and understanding how that changed his life instilled a fear that stayed with me. At 40, I was facing the same challenge that I had once lived with my dad. But I also had a survivor's instinct: I saw what he had done at age 57 to keep going. He was a fighter, and I am my father's daughter. I will fight.

> *Limits, like fears, are often just an illusion... Get up and never give up.*
>
> — **Catherine Kontos**

I sat in the cemetery remembering that at age 15 I had thought: *This can never happen to me.* But here I was at his gravesite, asking for guidance because I was an example of history repeating itself; and he would know what to do. As I sat sobbing, the clarity I sought finally came: I knew what I needed to do. Although he was gone, I could feel his presence. He was – and always will be – my guardian angel. My father was a dreamer and an explorer, even at 74 when he passed. He taught me "the secret" of youth.

> *We don't stop dreaming and exploring because we get old; we get old because we stop dreaming and exploring.*
>
> — **Catherine Kontos**

Just like that, I decided to close the business. It was a decision that would anger and disappoint many. No one more than me. I got threats, my car was vandalized, my equipment was stolen, and I was scolded for my "failure". Although I was full of fear and anxiety, I persevered with what I knew was the only thing to do. When the business closed, I was left with a mess. Nobody expected me to shut down. All the money was lost. But I had no choice. It was my business or my life. I chose life.

Now I was left with this Goliath building, and it needed to sell quickly to minimize the loss. I put it up for sale. After several months and no interest, I had to reach in my pocket and pay all the expenses of this dreaded place. Every time I was there, I would shake from the rush of memories and negative emotions. Who would have thought that in such a short time I could incur so much psychological and financial damage? Every day felt like an eternity. Each time I walked in, it was like a nightmare. I hated it.

My symptoms began to subside, but my sadness continued throughout the summer. My way of dealing with sadness was to get together with friends and family, occupying my mind with social gatherings. No matter how sad I was, my interaction with others was crucial to my well-being. I would force myself up. I would force myself out. I considered this a strength. I needed the distraction. Although it may have not been the best way to cope, it did get me through; it was what I needed at the time.

My daughter was my priority: taking care of her and my "duties" were always at the forefront. I cooked, shopped for groceries, read bedtime stories, ran to all her activities. I did whatever I needed to do to make sure my daughter and everyone else at home were well taken care of. All the while I functioned on a superficial level, but the deepest part of me was upset and angry for allowing all this to happen. I really did not love myself at that time. In my mind, I was a disappointment. I had been so stupid. I was everything negative. So many mistakes. How could I have been so naïve? I was a functional depressive. I was asked, "How could it go so wrong so fast?" "What did you do wrong?" On several occasions I was even asked, "How stupid are you?"

I tried to shield myself from the pain…the very deep pain that I was trying to hide. Spiraling into an ever-deeper depression, everything continued to unravel, including my marriage. From the outside looking in, no one would know we were falling apart. Only the people closest to me could see I was suffering. They saw through my meek attempts to smile; they knew I was covering up my pain. By the end of the summer, there was nothing but broken glass, and it was cutting me deep. My marriage, like a cracked vase, was irreparably damaged.

Forgive yourself for not knowing what you didn't know before.

– Catherine Kontos

Chapter Three

Shock and Earthquake

Never let life's earthquake shake your peace. Stay grounded.

– Catherine Kontos

My "Killer" Instinct

I had been in excellent shape, so much so that doctors were impressed enough to say that I was more fit than a 28-year-old. At least that is what they told me. So how does a vibrant, active, and seemingly healthy 40-year-old end up with a rapidly growing malignancy pushing her along the path of death?

It was 4 p.m. on August 26th, 2013, as I lay on the dark burgundy leather couch in the family room, the sun dappling through the patio doors where my feet lay dangling off the couch. As I watched a talk show, my hand brushed over my right breast. I immediately felt a lump popping up: as I lay horizontally, it floated more to the top.

This was, of course, frightening. I had felt lumps before, but the more I touched this one, the more it felt different than the others. I picked up the phone and walked out to my backyard patio to get some air. As I sat on a chair by my table, I dialed the number to the private breast clinic. To my surprise, I got an appointment to see the doctor the next day. Of course, I was trying to convince myself, it was nothing.

This wasn't nothing… I knew it was something. The next day, I went to the clinic, and the tests began. First came the mammogram. Mammograms were nothing new to me; I had undergone such a test one year prior. I then saw the doctor in his office. He told me nothing appeared on the mammogram. Nothing? How could that be? He then examined me and felt the lump. He insisted on an ultrasound and, of course, I complied. I lay in the dark on the clinic bed as the light shone from the monitor screen. The doctor went over my breast with the ultrasound and was able to identify the lump. He decided that we would need a biopsy to confirm whether it was a benign or malignant tumor.

As he continued to examine the side of my breast towards my armpit, I prayed that he would not find anything more. Everything, time and space – even my breath – was suspended in slow motion. Every move of his hand, every blink, pupils dilating… I noticed and felt everything. His breathing seemed louder to me. Both his and the nurse's voices suddenly seemed to crack ever so slightly. I could feel the tension. He didn't have to say anything: I knew the answer. I closed my eyes and waited to hear his verdict: there was another tumor growing in my lymph nodes. He informed me that a biopsy would be necessary in both areas. I had only two choices, and running away was not one of them: I could go through the private system, where I'd have an answer with 98% accuracy within one hour and 100% accuracy within 48 hours. Or I could go through the public system, where it would take three weeks to get an answer.

The choice was obvious. I valued my peace of mind, so I chose to go private. I went for dinner at a local pizzeria and returned an hour later. To my surprise when the results came back, the doctor told me all looked clear and I should not worry anymore. I felt relief, but my gut was telling me something different. I chose to think it was just fear and ignored it.

I went home, and a friend called me to go to a local bistro for a drink. After the day that I was having, I sure wanted a drink, so I met her and another friend. They were seated on barstools around a cruiser table, and I stood behind one of the stools listening to the conversation but contributing very little. I didn't mention a thing so as not to worry them. But my mind was a million miles away. I also wasn't feeling great. I felt I was suffocating, lightheaded, dizzy... so dizzy that I could barely get the words out, "I don't feel well."

It felt like the walls were closing in on me. I put my head down over my hands on the backrest of the chair. Suddenly, I started to come around again, but I was on the floor hearing voices over me say, "Get her water. Get her something for her head." I had passed out briefly. I'm not sure what happened and although disturbed by this event, I lay there and just started laughing. I couldn't believe I was on the restaurant floor. No one knew that I had just been through a very stressful day waiting for results that could change my life. I called my family, and I was driven to the safety of my home. I went to bed by myself, feeling scared and alone, hurt and insignificant. I had no one by my side.

> *Never take for granted a person who invests their time or trust in you. With love, compassion, patience and tolerance, you can never go wrong.*
>
> – **Catherine Kontos**

Two days later while I was driving, my cell phone rang. It was the doctor. He asked me what I was doing. I said, "I'm driving." He informed me that the pathologist had found atypical cells in my breast tissue, and he advised me to have surgery to remove them because they could eventually become cancer. I immediately agreed to go forward with the surgery. I was booked for September 11th, not a good date in my mind considering its history, but I found it was quite quick given that most patients must wait months for a surgery date.

On September 10th, I went for my preoperative appointment, where the doctor placed wires while looking at an ultrasound inside my breast in order to know exactly where he would cut. I asked him to cut under the breast or as far under as possible so the scar would not be so obvious. He agreed. It was really important for me that I would not have a scar on my breast, considering it was just a preventative procedure.

I spent the next 24 hours with wires in my breast, but this didn't stop me from going out for dinner that night. Apparently, this would become a recurring theme throughout my story. I guess it was my coping mechanism to just keep going on with my life, no matter the circumstance. If I kept myself distracted, then my mind would not go to that dark place where fear lives.

As the date approached, my fears started settling in. My biggest fear was to go under anesthesia. What if I was one of those people who doesn't wake up or who has permanent memory loss? This was my first time going under, so I didn't know what to expect. I asked whether I could be awake but heavily sedated. The doctor refused. On the day of surgery, I was filled with fear. I changed into a hospital gown and went into the surgical unit. I was naked under a single white sheet. I looked around at the equipment and began to pray and meditate as I always did to calm myself. Slowly, my fear subsided.

As I waited for the anesthesia to be administered, I accepted my circumstance, looked up, and opted for faith over fear. As the anesthesia was injected, the anesthesiologist told me to think of my perfect place. I closed my eyes, allowing my thoughts to wander: *Mmmmmm I can smell the salty air, the soft wind blowing on my face and the calming sound of the waves crashing onto the rocks.*

It didn't take long, just a few seconds, and the anesthetic took over. I fell into what seemed like a peaceful sleep.

Beyond the Scar

Upon waking in the recovery room, the first thing I felt was a heaviness in my chest. I opened my eyes: I was surrounded by light blue hospital curtains. Drowsy and in a great deal of pain, I immediately asked for morphine and to see my family. I looked over and saw my blood pressure was really low. It was 87 over 52. Normal is 120 over 80. The nurses came over and told me they would keep me until my blood pressure rose.

As I became more alert, the general pain in my chest area began to subside. I felt the pain: curiously, it wasn't coming from under the breast, but from the top right side. I placed my hand over the center of my breast, but there were no bandages there; instead I felt them on the top right side of my breast. This was all so confusing as I thought: *No...no!!! What happened?*

My mind filled with rage and I began screaming: "What happened? He was supposed to cut under my breast. We had an understanding!" My body had been violated; my rights had been violated; I felt betrayed. All I could think was: *Where's the doctor; I need to see the doctor; Right now! I was under, and he did what he wanted!?! He did not have permission to cut me up this way. We had an agreement! This is my body!*

The nurse informed me that the doctor had left. I burned with rage and couldn't stop crying. I was in a state of shock. My blood pressure rose to the point where it was now abnormally high. None of it mattered. I needed answers. I needed to deal with this.

As weak as I was, I demanded to be taken to his private office downtown to confront him. As I walked, I was steadied by my mom on one side and by another family member on the other side. We arrived on the 10th floor of the office building close to 6 p.m. The lights were off, and cleaners were mopping the floors. I noticed one of the office assistants walking towards the elevator. Sobbing, I told her the situation. She called the doctor on his cell phone and handed it to me. I reminded him of our agreement as to how he would proceed with the surgery. He calmly responded, "I had no choice, Catherine. I'm sorry, but there was no other way to get it all out and do it properly."

Miserable, I hung up on him and was carried to the car where I collapsed into the passenger seat. Never had I considered that if he found cancer in me, he would do what was needed to do to make sure it was all out. I had gone in for a preventative procedure that turned out to be life-saving surgery. I needed time to come to terms with everything that had happened to my body in such a short time. The fact was that this doctor had just saved my life, and I had no idea.

A few days passed, and the bandages started peeling off. As the last bandage fell off, I summoned the courage to look in the mirror. A sense of fear of what I was about to see overcame my body. I stood in front of the closet door mirror looking down on the floor for a few seconds, thinking: *I don't want to look. I don't want to look.*

With great apprehension, I took a few breaths and slowly got the courage to look up at my newly scarred breast. With my mouth open wide, I sobbed on and on and on. It hit me hard as I mourned the loss of my old breast. This is my new breast. This scar on my breast was very raw: real, red, and irrefutably permanent.

Understand my frame of mind at this point. I had been put under anesthesia with the understanding that this preventative procedure would leave me with a small incision: a slight scar – not very visible, – under the breast. It didn't go that way, and I had to come to terms with the fact that I woke up with a visible scar that – like it or not – would belong to me forever. I had to make peace with that, but it was still all too raw, fresh, surreal.

The breast is a part of my femininity, my sexuality, my identity as a woman. Now in my eyes, I was no longer attractive in that way. Before the operation, my breasts had been perfect; now I had this ugly scar. So I mourned. I mourned the loss of my once perfect breasts and my womanhood. The truth was that this would turn out to be the least of my worries. You know that saying, "Things could always be worse." The worst was yet to come, and my feeling about this scar would very soon become irrelevant in the big picture of life. Not to say that I did not have the right to feel that way. No one's pain or reaction should be compared to another's or minimized.

This was a great loss to me, and I had to go through several phases to come to grips with it. First, I had to overcome feelings of betrayal, whether real or imagined. Initially, I felt betrayed by the outcome. The scar on my breast challenged how I identified as a woman, and I needed people to understand this and support me as I grieved, so I could move on. We all have different experiences throughout our lives, and our perspectives are different from one another's. We all have a right to feel without being judged.

Nobody wants their emotions diminished. What they want to hear is: "I see how painful this is for you. I'm sorry you are going through this. Is there anything I can do to help?"

These three sentences are key to almost any situation. Often, it is hard to know what to say in difficult situations, like sickness or death. People get nervous and make the most inappropriate comments. Sometimes there simply are no words. Sometimes a hug is all anyone needs. Sometimes feeling safe from judgment is all anyone needs. Love them. Feel their pain. Be compassionate and just be present for them. That is what support is… simple, unconditional, and free from assumption and judgment.

Take a few seconds before passing your judgment on another. Take a few seconds and think of the impact it might make on that person's state of well-being. Be kind and gentle with your word, because you don't know what that other person is living right now, nor do you know how they got to where they are today. Your words and actions are the difference between someone hurting or smiling. Choose wisely and be kind.

– **Catherine Kontos**

A couple of weeks later, I got called in to discuss the pathology of the mass that had been removed from my body. Usually they just confirm the pathology and tell you if there's any follow-up.

No Escaping Fear

"Just die already"

Imagine being told those words? When I heard those words, I froze. They would come to haunt me for days, months, and years.

> *Words can spark happiness. Words can burn one's spirit.*
>
> – **Catherine Kontos**

I drove myself to the appointment the next day but asked my mom and another family member to accompany me. My mom stayed in the waiting room as I and a relative faced the doctor in front of his wooden desk full of files and papers. With his glasses perched on the bridge of his nose, the doctor's eyes pierced the document in front of him. My life felt as if it was in suspension as I waited for him to read the results. Why was I so nervous? It was just a routine follow-up after surgery... I noticed his face was somber as he uttered the words no one wants to hear: "The pathology found cancer cells in the tumor they removed from your breast. Right now, it's a Stage 2 triple negative breast cancer, but Grade 3 aggressiveness and speed of growth."

Grade 3 is the highest level, he explained. I was dealing with a monster. While he continued looking down at the paper, my body went numb. I looked at him dumbfounded and asked him, "How can this be possible? The biopsy did not show any cancer."

He replied: "I'm not sure what happened, but the results are clear; you have cancer."

I replied with deep consternation in my voice: "I'm 40. I exercise, I eat well… No breast cancer in my family ever. How can this be? I do everything right!"

I raised my arms in the air, looked up and said as if taking my last breath: "I give up."

At that moment, I realized that any sense of control I ever thought I might have had dissolved. I let go of all control. I did not know at that time how much that train of thought would help me through my cancer journey.

The words I had heard the night before – "Just die already…" – came rushing through my mind. I repeated it aloud a second time for everyone to hear, emphasizing each word in a louder, more angry and sadder voice: "I... HAVE... CANCER!"

Until that moment, I had not yet shed a tear. I was thinking: *It's okay. It's only Stage 2. As long as I don't have to do chemo, I'll get through this.*

Drugs and I don't get along. I am hyperreactive to most medications, that one-in-a-million patient who suffers side effects. A doctor once explained to me that I was likely missing an enzyme, which explains my intense reaction to medication.

Case in point: I once started a typical and routine treatment for acid reflux. The pill slowed down my digestion so much that I was diagnosed with gastroparesis, an irreversible disease involving paralysis of the stomach. When diagnosed, I had already lost 10 pounds in two weeks. Food was remaining in my stomach and rotting there. I remember vomiting the sandwich from the day before. The meal came out the way I had swallowed it the day before. Peppers and everything else came out undigested.

I started eating two to three cashews every 30 minutes, to keep some weight and prevent starvation. That's all I could handle. My doctor at that time told me to take a motility drug to speed my digestion. If that didn't work, I would need to be tube-fed for the rest of my life. I remember looking at the doctor and telling him that I was certain it was my body hyper-reacting to the medication. He insisted that was impossible and that gastroparesis was irreversible. He then gave me the motility pill to start treatment. I never took it and I stopped taking the other pills I had been prescribed by him as well, which I felt had caused my latest ailment.

I know that it takes two months for any medication to be removed completely from the body. So I waited, and then requested to be tested again. The doctor persisted in trying to convince me that there was no point to retest, but I insisted. We ran the test, and a couple of weeks later he opened his file, smiled and said to me: "So happy your stomach is working normally versus only 20% motility before. I'm glad to see the motility drugs are working."

I stood up, faced the doctor and told him: "Not only did I not ever start the motility pills, I also stopped taking the original pill that I told you was the likely cause of the paralysis."

He looked at me dumbfounded with his mouth open and in a seeming panic asked: "How is this possible? The pharmaceutical rep never told me of this side effect."

I slapped a few research papers in front of him that I had found online which proved that these drugs do slow down digestion in some more than others. I told him he needed to speak to his pharmaceutical representative and that I would report what happened to me to the pharmaceutical company. That was how it came to be reported as a possible side effect. At least this doctor didn't tell me I need antidepressants as had one of the doctors I had seen at a clinic during my symptomatic phase who had suggested my digestive issues were psychosomatic. That doctor got a nice letter after my discovery, proving I was not psychosomatic.

I came to the realization at that point that doctors can sometimes help you get better – maybe even save your life – but you need to trust yourself and listen to what your body is telling you. Really listen and don't be afraid to speak out about what you are feeling and about your treatment. A good doctor will listen and respect your opinion. Work with them and do what you need to heal your mind and body. I did it then, and now with my cancer diagnosis, I was going to do it again.

This was the reason why I was so terrified of chemo infusions. I didn't think cancer would kill me, but I was terrified that the chemo would. I looked at the doctor and asked him – actually stated to him – "I won't need chemo, right? It's only Stage 2."

He looked at me and said: "Well first, we need to get you back to surgery because there was a mass in your lymph nodes. We need to remove any that are possibly affected. Once you heal from that you will undergo chemotherapy and radiation. That's a guarantee. I will be meeting with other doctors to set up your treatment plan."

Suddenly everything blurred. His words, his motions… It felt surreal, like I was watching from the outside, looking at the doctor in slow motion. It felt as though time had stopped like in a dream. Suddenly my entire body started trembling. A heavy pressure weighed on my chest. I couldn't breathe… My next exhalation was a wailing, uncontrollable cry. In my mind, all I kept thinking: *This can't be happening... Please God: No!*

My head shook left to right. I could no longer hear anything being said. All I felt was pain in my gut, my heart. Fear overcame my entire body. I didn't understand how I went from not having cancer to having Stage 2 cancer. I kept repeatedly thinking: *Who screwed up? Is this a joke? Is it a mistake? No, it can't be. Please God, no. I am going to die. I am going to die. My baby girl. I can't die. Please God, she needs me.*

Shock and Daze

Leaving his office, I continued crying. As I approached my mom in the hallway, she was on the phone, speaking my brother's name. She looked up at me, her eyes welling with tears. She knew even before I could tell her that it was bad news. Her face flushed as she slowly lowered the phone away from her face. *(As I write this, my entire body is trembling, the memory and emotions are so vivid.)*

Looking at me with puzzled concern, she asked in Greek: "What's wrong? What happened?" (*Τι έγινε; Τι έχεις;*) Still in shock and crying, I uttered the dreaded words: "Mama, I have cancer. I have cancer." (*Μαμά, έχω καρκίνο. Έχω καρκίνο.*)

I saw her lift the phone back to her ear and in panic, she repeated to my brother in Greek: "She has cancer. She has cancer. I don't know. I don't know. I have to go." (*Έχει καρκίνο. Έχει καρκίνο. Δεν ξέρω. Δεν ξέρω. Πρέπει να σ 'αφήσω.*)

I walked past her to sit. Everything suddenly became so administrative, so clinical. They led me to an office waiting room full of people. I felt like I was in the middle of a funnel. Everything and everyone around me were just blurred objects. The secretary began booking my appointments with different doctors, therapists... I sat, crying uncontrollably. Everyone stared at me, but I didn't care who saw me crying. I wondered what I was doing there during such an intense emotional state. I should be alone with my family, and all this administrative stuff should be coming to me. As I sat there sobbing, an older woman came up to me. She kneeled, touched my knee, looked me in the eye and told me in French, "You will be fine. It'll be OK." (*Tout ira bien. Ce sera bien.*)

After what felt like hours, I was given papers – the beginning of this crazy new life called "cancer". But now, I needed to be alone. Hesitantly my family agreed, and my mom got a ride home. I cried for an hour. I felt stoned, numb. Soon after I got in my car, I got a call from a friend. She was her usual perky self, asking excitedly, "Hey Cat! How are you?" I casually answered: "Not well…" Not even thinking, I continued, "I was just diagnosed with cancer."

She started screaming: "What?!?! "What?!?! Nooooooo." Typical of me, I immediately blocked my own emotions to take care of my friend, who was wailing uncontrollably over my Bluetooth as I drove away. I calmed her down, realizing at that moment that everyone around me would need consoling: I put my feelings aside – something I had mastered in my life. It truly did not serve my well-being.

Looking back on this attribute of mine, I wonder whether I thought my feelings were less important. Why did I not matter to myself? I was in shock, and my instinct was to comfort others when I saw them hurting. I know that pain too well, and I never want others to feel it. I'll explain.

My family had suffered a terrible loss. My cousin who carried the same name as me (we both bore our grandmother's name) had passed away less than a year and a half prior to my diagnosis. She had contracted the most aggressive form of leukemia known as AML, what I called a freaky twist of nature that invaded her body. A cancer that should have killed her within weeks, she was able to fight for two years. She even got a bone marrow transplant. It was truly a miracle that she lived so long. We were all praying she'd survive it and lead a long, normal life.

In February 2012, although cancer-free, she passed away due to three infections invading her weakened body simultaneously. I had lost my mentor. We, the family, had lost our most loved Catherine Kontos, the first to get cancer and to die from it at the age of 51. So fresh in all of our minds, including mine, and my child's. It tore us apart.

Now I, the younger Catherine Kontos, had breast cancer. I remember when my cousin was diagnosed, I am not sure why, but I questioned God if he had chosen the right Catherine. I felt guilty. Ever since I was a kid, I had this fear that I would get terribly sick. It was more than fear, it was an intuition, and so when she got it, I had to wonder if it was all a terrible mistake. Well, whether God did or didn't make a mistake, both of us were eventually struck with cancer.

I knew that telling my family I had cancer would be the hardest thing I would ever have to do. Especially difficult would be telling my daughter, Nikki. All she knew about cancer was that her most beloved aunt had just been taken by it. No doubt she would immediately fear it would kill me too. So I drove, praying for strength. Strength to cope with everyone's reaction. Strength to cope and fight. Strength to not let despair interfere with my fight.

I drove and drove only to find myself at my father's grave once again. As mentioned, he had passed in 2009 before cancer and death had struck the Kontos family. This, without exaggeration, would have killed my father. He was the most empathetic and sensitive man I had ever known, to a fault. I went and sat once again in front of his grave. I cried, sobbing out loud: "Daddy, I have cancer. Please keep me safe. Talk to Him and ask Him to let me stay here a little longer."

I stared at the tomb for a while. I gathered my thoughts, stood up, and decided to be strong. Not sure how I was going to do it, but It was important to me to be strong for my daughter's sake. I needed to fight to stay alive no matter what.

For the next 48 hours, I shared the sad news with my family, consoling every one of them. I think the most disappointing and surprising reaction was when I called my cleaning lady to let her know that I would need her to sanitize my room more than usual because I had cancer. I heard her catch her breath, and then she hung up on me. I never heard back from her. That I will never understand, but it made me realize that some people can't handle that type of news, perhaps because someone really close to them passed. I guess some people just want to block those triggers. I'm not sure. Either way, it unsettled me.

> *Perception makes all the difference. Whether their views are based on experiences that triggered fear, love or hatred, their perspective is now altered and their thoughts and behavior become reactions to that altered state, and that pattern is very difficult – almost impossible – to change.*
>
> **– Catherine Kontos**

My family was still trying to rebound from the loss of my cousin, which was fresh. So even though no one said so to me, of course they were worried that if one Catherine Kontos didn't beat it, then the next Catherine Kontos would not either. That kind of fear can't be hidden. As each family member learned of the news, I repeatedly told them, "I'm not going to die. Don't be scared. I'll be fine."

I had no idea how serious my condition was. My second surgery revealed that my lymph nodes were also affected. This raised me to Stage 3 cancer. I was also informed that triple negative breast cancer is one of the most aggressive forms of cancer and that mine was growing at a rate of 70%. It is a type of breast cancer for which there is no proven treatment yet. The treatment and drugs they give you can be hit or miss. Cross your fingers and hope it's a hit.

My doctors orchestrated a very aggressive treatment to save my life. I was told that the reason for my misdiagnosis was because the pathologist had "never seen anything like it" when he looked at the biopsy report. The tumor was like a Twizzler, – part fibrosis, part cancer. Usually, cancer eats its way out, but not in my case. It was like my body was setting up roadblocks to stop it from growing. So, when the doctor pricked me with the needle on the side of my breast three times, he never hit the cancer cells, just the fibrosis.

As I awaited surgery to remove my infected lymph nodes, I could not stop thinking about the monster growing inside me. I awoke knowing it's another day that this creature was eating away at me. Dealing with this; sadness had overcome me, but it didn't stop me from living. There were things I needed to take care of, and that's exactly what I did.

My Journal in Real-Time

October 5th, 2013

Today is a Saturday. Usually, we'd be out, but I am home recovering from my second surgery. I'm feeling sad and anxious. I feel like I'm in a dark place tonight.

Today, most of the day, I felt weak. Slept in 'til 10:30. Struggled to get out of bed. Went for a walk with my girl around the circle. That was my highlight today. It was a sunny warm fall day.

I decided I was strong enough to start cooking today. I made Nikki's favorite, salmon tartare. I also made homemade poutine and bok choy. It took a couple of hours. I felt frustrated. I did not enjoy it. Usually, I enjoy cooking. I think I did a little too much. Nikki enjoyed the tartare. That made me happy.

Frank (my brother) came over. We watched a really bad comedy that Frank found hilarious. He has such a funny and different sense of humor than me. It was nice sitting with my mom and Frank. He's been coming around a lot more. Calling me more. He's scared. I could tell. So am I.

My mom told me that the priest prayed for me at church today. It's so nice to know that there are so many people praying for me. This is why I have faith that I will get better. I'm strong, both mind and body, and I feel I will not only make it but propel. I'm very blessed to have so many people love me. Popi and thia Lulu sent me an arranged fruit basket today like Toni had a couple of weeks ago. Yesterday, another friend dropped off a lavender gift. I feel loved.

I hate being home all day. I need to be around people.

Anxiety scale: 6.5

Depression scale: 7

Fatigue: 9

Symptoms: burning tongue, burning forehead, fatigue, numbness in arm from surgery.

October 6th, 2013

Overnight I was in a lot of pain but did much better through the day. My symptoms, besides the pain overnight, were a burning forehead, foot heel, and tongue.

Anxiety: 8.5

Depression: 7

I took my pain meds and kind of meditated to help me relax; all symptoms eventually subsided, and I fell asleep.

I woke up feeling better. I took one more med. I slept again in the morning. Got up, had lunch with mom and Nikki, and then the girls went for the first annual walk for the mission brewery.

I met up with them for the party. It was nice to see Father. He gave everyone a bible. Such a nice man.

October 9th, 2013

A couple of days ago I cleaned my office. Nothing on the bureau. Yesterday, I go to charge my portable. I see a church booklet face down. I turn it around and its Saint-Nectarios. This is the saint for illness and suffering. This booklet was given to me by my cousin Cathy a couple of weeks before her death. How did this book appear suddenly? I freaked...

Meanwhile, my client contacted me. I was so overwhelmed with emotion that he's well that I've been crying and thanking God for giving me the peace I've been longing for the past six months. If I saved this one life then it was all worth it. I'm so happy and at peace with it all now. Thank you, Lord.

Anxiety: 3

Depression: 3

Symptoms: Nausea after cappuccino, twitches, burning tongue.

Info: 4 fresh garlic cloves a day helps prevent breast cancer.

October 10th, 2013

Final results come in next week. I believe in prayer. I believe in miracles. I believe I will surpass and be well, and God will restore my health. I will thrive. I'm at peace with a lot, but I'm very emotional because I'm overwhelmed by everyone's love and support.

Time to get ready for the fight. It's been a long road, and it will be a long road, but it'll come and go like anything else, and I will be better than ever.

My dear lord and guardian angels, thank you for watching over me. I love you.

A tube was inserted into the side of my breast. It hung from the side of my waist to drain and empty into a small plastic bottle after the surgery. I had an event coming up in two days that I absolutely did not want to miss. It was an anniversary celebration, a night of dancing; and anyone who knows me knows I don't like to miss out on dancing and singing along to my favorite songs! Whether it's on a dance floor, or in my car singing like a nut while people in passing cars stare at me thinking: *What a happy person or wow, she has to be crazy...*

Either one is fine because a little crazy is what makes life fun! So, what's a girl to do? How was I to get dressed and not have this tube and bottle show? This could be a very embarrassing wardrobe malfunction. Can you imagine the horror of a bottle hanging out on the side? Knowing my character, I would turn it into a joke and say, "Shooters anyone?"

Well, I had to be creative. I went into my closet, looked at my clothes and improvised. I chose a purple strapless top. It was a heart-shaped bustier that opens at the waist like a skirt. That's where the bottle would hide. I tucked it in into my tights, and voilà! Nothing showed.

I went to the opening, socialized, danced and forgot about the bottle hanging on my side and the surgery, at least for that one night. It was a beautiful night, and it showed me that everything can be figured out; if I want something badly enough, I can make it happen. I had such a good time, in spite of what was happening to me. I could have come up with a million excuses, and I had good reason to miss it, but I decided that day that I am not a prisoner of life's obstacles. Instead, I challenge life when obstacles appear. It was my way of saying, "Damn you. You aren't stopping me. Bring it on." And boy did life bring it on!

Life will always have its challenges. As one passes, another one appears. Live through those challenges on your terms. They are there to teach you, to help you grow. Grow with gratitude, for these are lessons and gifts they give you. Know that the challenges are your blessings to all the good that already exists in your life. That's when you will understand and know you have it all.

– Catherine Kontos

October 12th, 2013

I didn't cry once yesterday. That's a good sign.

I'm feeling less pain than usual. I hate telling people. It just brings me down. Anyway, not too many people left to tell. I just don't want it to be real, and every time I say it, it's like an admission to my illness, and reality hits hard. I like feeling optimistic. I don't think I'll be telling others anymore.

I know when they know. They look at me differently. They speak to me differently. I see it, especially in their eyes. The sadness for me. It hurts others to see me and I don't even look sick. What's going to happen when I look sick?

We are going out tonight to celebrate the one-year anniversary. I hope I can make it through the night. It's important for me to be there tonight. If not, I would never go. My body is not strong enough, but I will push myself to be there.

Anxiety: 4

Depression: 4

Cry: once

Symptoms: twitches when falling asleep, my mouth tick makes my tongue burn, still hurting.

Fatigue: 6.5

October 13th, 2013

I woke up crying again today. I don't do it for long. It's little spurts as I wake up. I hate that though. I was angry today. How is it possible to be as thorough as I am with my health, but yet this was missed? I was at the clinic last year. Mammogram and ultrasound were done. I don't get it.

I got very tired last night. My will to live is so strong. I know this will help me surpass this.

I want to be an example of how you can have this and still live even thrive.

I just want to be able to endure all suffering and be able to be strong enough for my girl. After all this is done. I want to do as much as possible to help others cope with their illnesses.

Tomorrow I'm making lamb and potatoes. I invited the whole family to join us. I'm blessed to be always surrounded by loved ones.

Anxiety: 2

Depression: 2

Fatigue: 7

October 15th, 2013

Yesterday I had everybody over for Thanksgiving. Mom took care of everything. Anyway, it was still nice, but I was really tired. Frank got really choked up during prayer. He's scared. I did it to be thankful for everything God has given me. I appreciate all that I have. My baby girl, especially.

Fatigue: 8

Anxiety: 3

Depression: 5

Symptoms: pain, tongue burning.

Chapter Four

The Battles

Hurt is part of the journey. That's how you learn. The strongest people out there are the ones who laugh the hardest and adopt a genuine smile. They're the ones who have fought the toughest battles because they've decided they are not going to let anything hold them down. They are showing the world who's the boss. Keep smiling.

– Catherine Kontos

Flashbacks

Even though I seriously contemplated not telling her at all, I finally gathered the strength after a few days to tell my daughter, Nikki. I knew I would not be able to hide how sick I was, so I told her the truth. Understand that we are a BIG fat Greek family, and we had just lost four members in the family.

We are all very close and in each other's business. We love each other, whether we're distant cousins or brothers and sisters. We even refer to people as cousins when they are not – just because we spent so much time growing up in each other's homes. So any loss, whether it's an uncle or a close friend, we take hard because we love them like they were our own father or sister.

Nikki was very close to my dad, who passed suddenly from a massive heart attack while we were at *Disney* (the most magical place in the world) celebrating my daughter's 7th birthday.

On the evening before her birthday, we had a tradition to do something that we would never do again after. As we walked to our room, we were passing a pool. My childish instinct came over me: I looked at Nikki walking by my side and, with a smirk, said to her: "Nikki, it's almost midnight. What is the last thing you will ever do again as a 6-year old?" I lifted my eyebrows and nudged my face with a huge smile towards the pool. "Go for it. Jump in with your clothes on!"

Her face just lit up with excitement as she hustled to remove her shoes, ran towards the pool and jumped in with a scream, "Yeeeees!!!!"

A big splash sounded and down deep in the water Nikki went. As her head popped up with a big smile, she swam to the edge of the pool, and blurted out, "That was fun!"

Living in the moment and enjoying every precious minute is the fulfillment we crave. We never know as each day passes what will change. Within days, it did for us.

It was the 22nd of December. The number 22 is a number of great significance to me. I believe it represents my guardian angel – my dad. It always appears when something is happening in my life, when I feel uncertain. It's not necessarily a warning or an approval. It's a message that signifies that I'm on the right path. Good or bad, I have to continue that journey and to feel secure that I'm heading the right way. It helps me have faith.

That morning, at 1:30 a.m., I awoke from a deep sleep feeling nauseous; tossing and turning for about 20 to 30 minutes. The phone by my bedside rang a half ring and disconnected. I looked around the dark room with its two double beds and felt cold. Everybody was sound asleep. Under my breath, I said, "Ohhh, I feel really nauseous. I can't sleep…" The phone rang again. I sat up in my bed, answered it and heard my sister's trembling voice. As she began to speak, I knew… I just knew.

"Cath, I have some bad news. Dad just passed away."

"OK," I replied in a daze.

She continued: "He died of a massive heart attack and was declared dead about 30 minutes ago."

Again, I replied, "OK."

Confused by my reaction, she continued: "Cath, do you understand what I'm saying? Dad passed away."

I replied: "I know. We're coming home."

I got up, started pacing, threw a piece of luggage on the bed and started packing, all while on the phone trying to get six seats on the earliest plane out. My heart was racing and my hands were shaking. Everyone was crying. I was going through the motions, but I had yet to cry. I just knew I needed to get home.

My mom. My poor mom. I couldn't break down now. I needed to get organized and get everyone ready to go home quickly.

Meanwhile, I tried to gather the strength and words to tell my daughter, hoping I would not cry; convincing myself I was strong enough to tell her. I sat by her bedside, nudging her awake. I gently placed my hand over her forehead and brushed her hair away from her face. In a soft voice I began: "Hey baby girl, can you wake up for Mommy? You have to get up because we have to go soon."

She sat up. "What's wrong Mommy?" I replied: "It's

Papou." I just looked at her for a few seconds, then drew a deep breath and gently told her that her grandfather – the one she resembled who taught her to play chess at age 3, had passed away. "Papou is with the angels now. He passed away not too long ago. I'm so sorry baby."

I thought about how my dad and Nikki used to try to fool each other while playing chess. One would move the chess piece when the other was looking away from the game. Then they would start fighting, screaming, accusing each other of cheating. Playfully, of course. It was the funniest thing to watch. They loved each other, only the way a grandfather and granddaughter could.

There was the time he dressed up as Santa during one of Nikki's birthday parties, before Christmas. I told him, whatever you do, don't speak. Just say, "Ho, ho, ho." So here comes Santa in all his glory, with sunglasses. It was the funniest scene. He sits with Nikki on his lap and, of course, forgets that he was not supposed to speak.

Instead he turns to Nikki and asks her in his strong Greek accent: "Haylow: Wat eez yore name" – translation: "Hello: what is your name?" Nikki turns her head swiftly, looks at him with confusion in her eyes and starts telling him off… All we understood was, "Papou…" But as her hands gestured wildly, we knew she was thinking: *What the heck!* Everyone at the party laughed so hard we were crying. Unforgettable; my father truly was…

Now, as I told her he had died, she cried. That's when I teared too, but still kept my composure the best I could. I held her in my arms so tight. This news had just broken my baby's heart. She suddenly burst out: "Papou died on my birthday!"

The heartbreak was overwhelming, as it is when any parent passes. It's indescribable until you experience it. Suddenly the person who was there all your life is gone. It's a denial that stays with you for a very long time. The pain slowly eases over the years, but never truly leaves. A piece of you is forever missing.

Terror in Tears

By age 10, my daughter had already experienced enough trauma. Death seemed to be chasing us. Aunts and uncles, fathers and cousins, one by one, gone forever. Our family gatherings were now at funerals. The entire family was in a daze of depression, including my little girl. The one experience she had with cancer was the one where the person had died. Oh, how I wished I didn't have to tell her that her mom was so sick, that I could protect her from having to go through this with me. But there would be no way to hide it from her... plus it would feel like a betrayal of trust; I could not lie to her.

How do I stay strong when I am terrified myself? How do I tell her I have cancer and not scare her? How do I not fall apart when all I have been doing is crying? How???

The day that I broke the news to Nikki, I had been lying in bed and asked her to come lie with me. I gathered the courage and began telling her the fearful news that would reshape her young mind forever. This kind of news changes a person. Although we didn't know how Nikki would be changed, we knew for sure that she would no longer be the child with the vibrant, active and healthy mom, and I felt responsible. This is how cancer spreads beyond the stricken person, instilling fear in everyone you love. No shame or guilt. Cancer doesn't discriminate; it doesn't care. I just prayed I could sensitively break the news to soften the blow.

As I lay on my bed with a tortured mind, I looked at her and began: "I need to tell you something. Mommy is sick, but doctors told me I will get medication, and it will help me." She asked, "How are you sick Mommy?" I hesitated, my chest felt heavy: "Mommy has to take a lot of medication for the next little while, and that's going to make her look sick. You know a lot of people get sick these days, and they go through a tough time for a little bit, and then they get better like a few people we know."

I started naming people and asked rhetorically, "They are fine now, aren't they?" She looked confused and worried and answered, "Yes, Mommy." I continued, "Baby, I have it too." She asked, "Cancer, Mommy?" "Yes, but I will be okay. Just like all those other people." With tears falling, she stammered: "... but Thia Cathy."

I tried consoling her, "Baby, it's not like Thia Cathy. Don't get scared. I promise that Mommy will be OK. I promise." We both cried as I held her in my arms tight... so, so tight. I explained: "A lot of people get cancer. It's almost expected today, and they live. Do you understand? Mommy will just be sick for a little while because of the medication. I promise you; Mommy will be fine. There are different cancers, and not everyone dies. Some just get sick, and after a while, it passes."

I told her this with great conviction, and at that moment, I felt sure that I would not break my promise to her. She was the spark that always ignited the fight in me. The fight to persevere for a happier life. The fight to live. She made me a better person. Stronger.

I decided that this spark would forever burn away cancer and everything else that could hurt her or me. I knew, without a doubt, that cancer was just a symptom of the high-stress life I lived and that it would pass. It had invaded my body, so now I had an opportunity to cleanse it, as well as my soul from the anger and sadness that was eating away at me. Cancer would afford me the strength to fight all my demons at the same time. Cancer was forcing me to become a fierce fighter. I needed to fight for myself because I am worthy. I deserve to live.

And so, I made this I vow to myself: I would no longer allow fear to reside in me, nor would I be the puppet they all wanted me to be. I would live fiercely with my head held high – proud of my successes, accepting my failures as lessons. This child would have a mother who would be fully present and available – not only physically, but emotionally. I would not let her down. I was not going down.

Cancer invaded my body, but I would not let it take my soul. Something would die, but it wouldn't be me.

Thank you, Cancer. I am grateful. Thank you for your message. I am heeding the warning, but it's time for you to go. I am changing myself from the inside out, and there is no room for you to grow here.

We lay together, just holding each other as I stroked her hair. I could imagine the fear she must be feeling. Why did she need to suffer this anxiety that cancer brings? All I could ask for right now was that I could help this child feel hope, not fear. I asked whether she had friends who had cancer in their families. She told me she knew of a girl and she believed that her mom had recovered. I told her to take the time to speak to her at school for support.

The next day she went to school and shared the news with some friends. Her friend Catherine told her that both her grandmother and mother were survivors and not to worry, I would be a survivor too. When she came home and told me about her friend, her face was lit with hope, not fear. That consoled her and gave her some peace, just as I had hoped.

> *When life throws you a curveball, you take that bat and hit that ball with all your strength out of the ballpark.*
>
> – **Catherine Kontos**

The Worst of Times

Although I had convinced myself that I would live, that did not mean that I would not feel all the emotions of this torturous journey. Fear visited me often. I cried a lot during the first couple of months following my diagnosis. It felt as if black clouds were layered one over the other, keeping me lost under a whirlwind of dark, scary emotions that beat me down. I was never able to catch my breath before the next hit. Life was happening to me.

This meant life or death. All I kept wondering: *Would this be life's last and final hit? Would it be the one that would knock me out for good?* It was me against cancer. Cancer is a fierce fighter. It does not judge your life. It is ruthless, striking children, the good, the bad, the old, the pregnant – sucking the life out of any and all. Would cancer spare me, and if so, why? As months passed, I realized the many gifts that cancer could give me. But for now, fear was foremost in my heart and my soul. It consumed my mind.

In complete darkness, your eyes will automatically adjust to see.

— **Catherine Kontos**

Of all the things that come with cancer, I was most terrified of the chemotherapy. I mourned the loss of my health and the loss of my freedom. I would soon mourn the loss of my hair and my once perfect breasts.

October 16th, 2013

Today I woke up very tired. I brought Nikki to school, came back, and slept until 10 a.m. I then took my time to get ready. I slept crying and woke up crying. What makes me cry is that I feel like I can't be touched or kissed for a few months. That's so hard for me. I will miss that so much. I will beat this. I asked for an MRI. In case it's in my other breast. I need to make sure. If nothing shows up. I hope chemo will kill it. It has to. I'm contemplating a full mastectomy.

Fatigue: 7

Anxiety: 6

Depression: 4

Symptoms: pain, tongue burning

October 17th, 2013

Very hard to get out of bed. I was feeling fear all night long. I woke at 2:30 a.m. scared that this is going to be what kills me. I guess what the doctor told me scared me. I told my Uncle Timothy and he was speechless at first. Then he told me, "What God gives you, He can also take away." He also told me to keep praying and hoping, and God would listen. I went to the gym; that felt good but wasn't enough to cheer me up. Feeling some piercing pain from my underarm.

October 20th, 2013

I've been sad all weekend. Crying a lot. Why do I not love myself enough to accept this scar? This whole thing has rocked my world and especially my confidence.

Chapter Five

Whirlwind Survival

We sometimes make ourselves suffer because something in our life is not going the way we want. It's in those times we must let it be and just have faith that if it's meant to be, it'll be. Trust the journey.

– Catherine Kontos

Building from Rubble

It had been several months since I had closed my business. Every month that went by with this Goliath of a building, thousands of dollars were flying out the window, adding more stress on my marriage and me. I needed a business that would create revenue and require less of my physical presence. I came up with the idea of starting a vacation rental business, even though I had no clue about vacation rentals. The property that won my heart wasn't the average mountain cottage; it had nine bedrooms and nine bathrooms that I converted into an 11-bedroom estate for 30 guests. My first thought: *Who the hell will rent this place for so many people?*

I searched online and found there were a few big cottages, but none this big. I didn't know where to start, considering I had never been involved in this type of business. But I did know marketing, and I knew real estate. I spent the next few weeks building a new website myself and placing the chalet on different online advertising sites. All this on my laptop while in bed recovering from the surgeries and suffering from depression.

Little did I know that I had just tapped into a niche market and a business that would help me support the building for the next few years. People love reunions and parties: what better experience to have than to celebrate at this perfect chalet? I came up with a price point, promotions, and a marketing campaign.

As reservations started ramping up, so did my knowledge. I created contracts from scratch, calendars, email templates... Then I hired a cleaning crew and a property caretaker. All this from the comfort of my bed. Whenever I felt well enough, I would go up and meet with the caretaker, but to be honest, I hated going up to the chalet. Anxiety would overcome my body every time. Combine that with all my other emotions tied to cancer and a failing marriage; I'm not sure how I did it all.

The caretaker had been hired right before my chemotherapy started. I depended on him greatly. He was a godsend and a blessing over the next few years. I never had to worry. Another person could have easily taken advantage of the situation and made a nice paycheck. He stayed as the caretaker and property manager for the next few years.

We have all been victims of something. Some more than others. But there's no way in hell you should give into the victim mentality. You are not weak. You don't need sympathy. You made your choices, and some choices have been made for you. Either way, you have the option: bow down and blame others for the situation and continue a toxic relationship with yourself; or reclaim your power and rise because you are strong. Never fall into the trap of having others feeling sorry for you as your way of coping with heartache and tragedy. All you are doing is hurting yourself. You are the master of your life.

– Catherine Kontos

Renting the chalet to families and their friends was one of many ideas that would flush out all the bad vibes I felt in that place. It was my plan. My course of action: Flush the toxicity and fill it instead with the tonic of happiness and joy. I knew I had to kill the bad vibes in there and replace them with good ones. So what's the first thing any good Greek girl is going to do? Well, find a priest to bless it. That's what!

Next on my list: get happy events booked there to boost the positive energy that beautiful memories, laughter, and joy bring. As family and friends came in and out of the chalet, the bad energy started to fade. The chalet has since hosted reunions, including weddings, for people from all over the world. Even my caretaker ended his career at the chalet with his own wedding. A great way to finish his time at this beautiful place – a repository for people's beautiful memories. *This is the place I got married; Remember this place? This is where we all reunited after so many years.* They will look back and be filled with joy. How beautiful…

What was once a place that had caused me pain was now a place that created joy for many. I had people coming in from around the world to reunite with their loved ones. Dubai, Korea, England, the US – you name the country: we had them staying at my chalet. The fighter in me turned it around while I was sick and battling cancer.

Although the chalet was now infused with the joy of guests, it was not joyful for my heart or pocketbook. I had lost a lot of money. This huge debt would continue to stress me for a very long time. The rentals were not enough to offset the loss I had taken, and my savings were being depleted. Plus, all the repairs absorbed any profits I did make. This continued to be a reminder of my mistakes and "failures".

I decided to put it for sale…get rid of it and the reminders of what could have been. But it wasn't selling. It was a buyer's market, and the chalet was in no condition to be sold. So I thought rationally: *What activities had I been doing all these years with great success?* I had become great at buying and selling homes and businesses. I knew I needed to do the same thing here. I also knew I might go broke doing it. It needed a lot of work. I had already invested thousands upon thousands, but I needed to do more. So I took it off the market, and in the following months and years, I started rebuilding it piece by piece while still promoting it. This place needed a lot of TLC – from rebuilding the foundations to fixing retaining walls, roofs, balconies, and stairs.

I also needed to create a buzz, so I came up with the idea of a beach wedding at the lake. It would be the first of its kind at this lake. The possibility of this happening depended on the municipality. After three rejections, I decided one day to show up without an appointment to see the manager in charge of the beach. Thankfully he agreed to see me. I persevered until I got the one "yes" that I needed. The wedding party was approved, and it happened with over 100 people in attendance. It was perfect, even making a writeup in the local newspaper. The town declared it to be the most beautiful wedding ever.

Joining the local Chamber of Commerce was next on my list. I threw my business in a contest and won the public vote. What a feat! Once again, I made it into the local newspaper; and this time, I and the chalet were both featured. As the chalet's business grew, I attracted the attention of many. And as the years went by, more and more people were asking me to rent their chalets. So I started a vacation rental reservation agency. It comforted me to know that my initial failure and struggle were only a very crooked path to this idea that brings so much joy to so many people. All this came into existence from the comfort of my bed. Sick and scared, I soldiered on.

It goes to show you that when you put your mind to something, put a plan into action and do what needs to be done, things happen. Life was no longer happening to me. I was making life happen for me. Life's obstacles are there to challenge us. The challenges are there to teach us something, and if we are present enough to learn, we can grow. As difficult or as scary as they may be. Sometimes we try to push these challenges away. Have you noticed what happens? The more you focus on denying the challenge, the more unbearable and overwhelming it becomes until you finally take positive action.

So either the challenge will make you feel so uncomfortable that you will have no choice but to take action and make changes, or the challenge will simply defeat you. It doesn't matter how slow you move forward, as long as you are moving. Even if there are setbacks; your journey is not a race. It's yours. You make it the way you want it to be. No judgments. No comparison. Own your journey. It's your life. Your choices.

Even storms can be beautiful, but your fear of them changes your perspective.

– **Catherine Kontos**

During that time of surgeries, I received an email that put a smile on my face. It was from an old client of mine during a time when all I saw was darkness. I remember being told when I first met my client: "This guy is hopeless. He's scum. You will not be able to help him."

My response: "Any person who walks through my door into my care comes in as a new page. I do not judge them for their past, and I do not make assumptions about their future. If I can help him even 15%, that is 15% better than he's come in."

He told me in his email that he was doing really well, that he had reunited with his family and upon his return, he would be starting a new job. He thanked me in a most profound way that touched my heart. He told me that he believed that God placed him in my path, and I was the angel who finally helped him.

My eyes filled with tears and my heart grew full because even as I was going through the darkest moments of my life, I had a purpose. Months before, while I was lying in bed crying, asking God to make me sick, ready to end my life, something bigger than me was happening that I was unaware of... For the first time, a man had someone believe in him, and it impacted him in a way that kept him well and away from his disease.

> *Even in the darkest of moments, when everything seems so dark, something beautiful could be blossoming.*
>
> – **Catherine Kontos**

This moment of realization was what I would return to when I felt I was in a dark place. God has bigger plans. We just need to trust the journey and accept our faith. We don't always see the reason, and it might not even have anything to do with us. It's the butterfly effect with endless possibilities affecting many.

> *The dark moments in life will come but know that it's never completely dark. The light is there. You just have to have the will to look at it.*
>
> – **Catherine Kontos**

Hard as Stone

I felt like I needed to get mentally stronger for my cancer journey. I had been beaten up. I didn't know how I would face this with everything else going on in my life. My marriage spiraling, my business lost, my family devastated. How would I maintain the mental and emotional strength so that this journey would not break me? I needed to be stronger than it. I needed to kill it before it killed me.

I made decisions about how I would focus 100% of my attention and energy on knocking this cancer out. I needed to remove all noise, distractions, and upsets. Even though I was generally a very fit person, I had become physically and emotionally run down. There was no denying that my body was already weak and tired, and this was only the beginning. I understood that it is impossible to feel fear in a state of calm and relaxation; that's where I needed to be. So I decided to practice visualization, meditation, and mindfulness. My mind was running a marathon from morning to night, thinking of anything and everything. I needed to calm down. I thought the best thing to do would be to go to a retreat alone to find the peace I needed to visualize winning the fight.

I wanted a nearby place, but the one I found was yoga-centric from morning to night. That's not what I wanted. So I had to look further: I found a resort-style retreat in the Caribbean and decided to book on that Wednesday to leave that Friday. I had never traveled alone. I was a little nervous because I was not only traveling alone, but I was not well. I had just finished the surgeries and knew how common it was just to wake up suddenly and not be well. But in my mind, there was no choice because this trip was vital to my well-being throughout the treatment. So, I booked it.

My luck, the next day as I lay down to sleep, my entire abdomen started to seize and tighten, the pain spreading. I got a sudden sharp pain on my left backside; the pain intensified, becoming worse than labor pains. I was rushed to the closest ER. Doctors told me I had a kidney stone. I couldn't believe it. After everything, now I had to deal with a stone? What the hell!?!

I was given narcotics, and the pain subsided. They sent me home to let the stone pass on its own. So I went home drugged, and an hour later, the pain returned with a vengeance, even worse if that's possible! I returned to the hospital hunched over and moaning in agony like I was about to give birth. People stared, but I did not care. They placed me in a bed and ordered morphine. They informed me that it would take about an hour to get it and administer it to me. As I sat up on the hospital bed waiting for the morphine, the pain kept intensifying. I was grabbing at the railing, swinging it, screaming and crying, "Get me drugs!!! Get me drugs!!!"

The pain was so intense it cut my breath. I swear that contractions were nothing compared with this. The nurse finally came after an hour, which seemed like an eternity and administered the morphine intravenously. I lay down and waited for the pain to subside.

An hour went by. I heard the doctor come into my curtain-covered cubicle. He asked,

"How are you feeling?" Stoned, I looked at him with blurred vision, my thoughts formulating ever so slowly and said: "Doc, I am stoned like hell, but I can still feel pain."

He chuckled: "Wow, that much pain, huh...?"

They were administering the morphine every hour on the hour. I was flying high; the pain eventually subsided. They sent me home with a prescription for narcotics and was told once again that I would likely pass the stone on my own. A few weeks passed, and the pain never returned. The doctor told me he felt that the stone had passed, considering the pain had not returned. Well, that assumption about my stone almost cost me my life later on.

Needless to say, I canceled my trip, which had been scheduled for the next day. Can you imagine if I had gone south and been alone when this pain from the stone struck? I would have been so scared. As they say, everything happens for a reason. My bad luck seemed to chase me these days.

Chapter Six

Entering the Fire Zone

In stopping the tears, you also stop the water that feeds your growth.
Let the drops feed your soul.

– Catherine Kontos

Breathing in Calm

I had to learn to keep a calm mind, so I started with guided meditation. I visualized a powerful light (the chemotherapy) entering my body, killing all the cancer cells and expelling them. Other times I used Greek prayers. I put on my headphones, went online, and listened to the chanting voices of Greek monks. I felt the prayers resonating deep within my soul. I often fell asleep to these prayers, hoping my mind and soul would feel them and help me heal. It put me in a meditative state, providing me with the calm I needed.

I also needed to control the information fed to me. Usually I need to know everything about what, how, where, and when. But upon diagnosis of my cancer, I ceased all control. I knew that even though the medical system kept failing me with misdiagnoses or mistreatment, I still had to keep faith, trusting that the doctors and medicines would heal me. Yes, there are many natural ways of healing, just as there are many drug options.

Medicinal marijuana, a supersized dose of Vitamin C, fruits that will heal, herbs that will cure – the options are endless. Between searching online and hearing from concerned family and friends reaching out, I was overwhelmed. In fact, I broke down and decided enough with all the information and statistics. I was grateful for the outpouring of love and concern, but all that help and concern was drowning me. It was more information than my mind could handle. I was focused on coming to grips with what was happening to me. Knowing that a decision could mean life or death.

So I asked everyone, including my doctors, to stop. I did not want to know survival statistics because I already knew I was in trouble. I threw back the half-inch-thick book they gave me about the side effects of chemotherapy. I just wanted to know the critical symptoms – the ones that could kill me.

Sometimes less information really is better. I did not want to fill my head with symptoms I would likely not get and then live in fear with every ache that I felt. I didn't have control over much, but I could definitely take control of what feeds my mind.

Until a week before chemotherapy, I was convinced that the surgery had removed all my cancer. My blood tests never showed any cancer markers. So, I was trying to understand why I would need to do the chemotherapy if I no longer had cancer. I sat there arguing with my doctor. Don't forget, I wasn't worried about the cancer killing me. I was worried about the chemotherapy.

So I asked for one statistic to make my decision. "Doctor," I said, "what are the chances my cancer will return if I don't do the chemo?" He was staring at his papers: "Well, let's see…triple negative cancer. Highly aggressive. Growth rate at 70%. Stage 3 metastasis to lymph nodes." His conclusion: "I would say 50/50. You need to do this, Catherine. I'm strongly advising you to do this."

He was desperately searching for a "yes" from me. I looked him in the eye: "I'll do it, but know that the chemo might kill me. Please, I beg you to make sure that it is not too strong. I react badly to medication."

He looked at me and said, "You're young; we'll do our best to keep you safe."

As I prepared to leave, I noticed boxes with the skull and X symbolizing poison near the chemotherapy room. I remember looking at it and thinking: *That poison is going in me... God help me.*

I went home and prepared for death, pulling out my life insurance policy and last will and testament. I had accepted death. I had to.

Decision - Choosing Love over Fear

As my chemotherapy appointment approached, my prayers were rampant. I would stay in bed eyes closed, praying morning to night.

Please Lord, don't let this be it. My daughter... my daughter needs me. It's too early for me to go. She won't thrive without me. No one else can love her and take care of her like I do.

Then the negotiations and begging came. At first, I thought: *Let me live long enough to see her get married.* Then I thought: *Well maybe that's not the best deal. I want to live well into my 80s.* One thing I did feel was that cancer had been given to me for a reason. I had to make something positive out of the experience.

First, I needed to figure out why I got it. At first, I thought I was being punished for some reason. I was brought up thinking that if you did good, God would reward you, but if you did bad, God punished you. My first instinct was to believe that I was being punished for my sins. I even had a family member say this exact thing to me. That God was "rattling" me, "shaking" me up. That did not sit well with me. Consequently, guilt and sadness overcame me. *I'm a good person*, I thought. *I help others all the time. I give to charity. I do my best to be a great mom, daughter, sister, citizen, friend... Does that not make up for any sins I've committed? We are all sinners, so why me?* I remember dropping to my knees in my bedroom, bowing to the floor and begging for God to spare my life.

Screaming over and over again: "Why me? Why me? I'm sorry I asked for it. Please, I will never ask for it again. Please God, please forgive me. I will appreciate life. I will never take it for granted. I asked out of stupidity and desperation. Please, I will never do it again."

I continued: "I know I wasted most of my life being miserable and not being grateful. I wasted all that time. I promise I will make good on all of this. I will make a difference. I will live with gratitude. I will teach others to be grateful and never lose hope."

I sat there sobbing for hours until I fell asleep on the floor. When I awoke, I felt drained. It was as though the life had been sucked out of me. It took a day to recover from a breakdown of this magnitude; then I became fiercely focused. The pain and sorrow needed to be released so I could transform into a lioness.

Did my own fears cause me to attract this cancer? I got angry as I concluded that my way of thinking until then is what had caused me to live in fear all my life. Of course, I sinned; I'm human. It didn't mean God was punishing me. Are innocent babies plagued by sickness because God is punishing them? How ridiculous is that? What a horrible self-destructive way to think. To me, God is love. This wasn't God's way of punishing me. Cancer just happens. I believe that when certain ingredients of physical and emotional attributes combine, it creates a recipe for genes to mutate and transform healthy cells into cancer ones.

Another theory of mine is that in some instances, it is just pure bad luck. Was my mind so powerful that I had actually given it to myself? I know one thing: I lived in fear for many years. I would wake up and sleep in fear, my mind filled with anxiety, which transmitted to my body I didn't sleep well and always felt tired due to my mind never shutting off. I knew that this would eat away at me and eventually make me sick. Nobody can live that way. That's not a life.

November 20th, 2013

I had my first chemo. I tried to keep positive. I had moments where I beat my car and cried. When I was praying yesterday morning, I was crying hard, but praying so hard that I felt God. I opened my arms towards the sky, and it was almost like an out-of-body experience. I really felt His presence in me. There was a sense of peace that I have never experienced before. It was beautiful.

I was quiet most of the morning. I did the chemo under tremendous and unnecessary stress. I need peace in my life, not stress. We drove home. All I wanted to do is see my baby girl and hug her. She's my medicine. And I did. We went to her school. I got out of the car and went to the schoolyard and hugged her so hard.

The worst time to make important decisions is when you're in fear mode. Unless of course, you're in real fight-or-flight mode, like being chased by a bear in the forest. Prior to my cancer, most of my decisions were fear-based. I always expected doom; I focused on immediate consequences rather than the long-term effects of my decisions. Like most anxiety-prone sufferers, I expected the worst and tried to prepare for it, although most of us in that state of mind believe that we can prevent it from happening. But I wasn't happy always projecting into the future and imagining the worst. I needed to change this because I felt I had wasted 40 years being miserable and living a mediocre existence as a result. I asked God to give me a chance to live; I promised I would do so much good if I had another 40 years.

Suddenly, answers came rushing at me. For the first time, I had found some clarity even though I was in crisis.

First, I knew I had to end my marriage. The relationship was toxic, and it was time to let it go. I didn't know how or exactly when, but it had to be done. Next, there was no way I was going to go through this and not share my experience with others. I needed to teach, inspire and help others. I promised God I would. I had finally found my purpose. I just needed to get through the chemotherapy.

Then it hit me. I had asked to be sick, and I got sick. If my mind had that power that meant I was capable of manifesting my destiny. If I believed that to be true, then my strong will to be well would be my new destiny. Period. This had to become my new truth, and the laws of attraction would make it so, even if fear would make many attempts to deter me as you will see…

Day of Reckoning

Chemotherapy day arrived. A person who would resist taking even Tylenol was about to get a bomb injected in her. The drug of all drugs. I was deathly quiet heading to the hospital. I stopped at the church and said a quick prayer to keep me strong.

As I waited for my turn, silent, heavy tears escaped my eyes as if the demon had come to sweep my mind. Fear took over…

Would I survive today? I looked around the room. I was among patients ranging in age from their 20s to 70-plus. They were all waiting for their turn on the chair; some with hair, some with scarves, others with wigs and some rocking bald. Some looked very sick, while others looked like just any healthy person on the street. Which one would I be? The unknown is death to someone who suffers from anxiety. But this time, there was nothing I could do. No control.

I knew that keeping calm and relaxed was key. You see, you cannot feel fear if you are relaxed. It's physically impossible. So I breathed and brought myself into almost a meditative state. I blocked everything and everyone around me.

Suddenly I heard my name called. It was time. It was my turn. As the nurse walked me into the room, the first thing I saw was a nurse in her 20s with a long clear plastic shield covering from her face past her abdomen. It reminded me of a gas mask with a bulletproof vest worn by soldiers or riot police. This was definitely a war, but with chemicals. I thought: *Oh my God, what am I doing?*

Fear overtook me. What was I doing here? All around me were sick-looking people: some in beds and others in chairs getting infused. It was the saddest room I had ever been in. I felt like I was walking to my death. Just like a dream or more like a nightmare; it felt like the longest walk through an endless, dark alley.

Each step brought me closer to the moment I feared. My attention switched from one person to another, watching them get their poison medicine. Every detail was noticed. The look on their face. The sound of their voice. Most looked drowsy. Some even slept on the brown leather recliners. Since it was my first time, and they did not know my possible reaction to the chemotherapy, I was directed to a bed in a cubicle, away from the rest of the room. I sat with my feet dangling off the bed. The noises from the machines surrounding me, although faint, seemed deafening to me. I stared out the window and closed my eyes, soaking up the sunshine with my face and allowing the light to feed my soul.

Suddenly, I heard wheels rolling on the floor. As the noise grew louder, I opened my eyes and saw the nurse heading down the hallway, wheeling the chemotherapy pouch towards me. *Okay, this is it*, I said to myself.

She placed a cup in front of me containing six pills of different sizes "What is all this?" I asked. Her answer: "Mostly anti-nausea and corticosteroid pills. You will also be injected with Benadryl, in case you have a reaction to the chemo."

I stared at the pills as she walked away, I'm thinking: *I need to run. I need to leave now. I don't have to do this. I can't do this. I'll leave and go straight to the airport and leave. I can't do this. I can't.*

I started to cry and told the returning nurse: "I can't do this. I'm scared. I can't."

She tried to comfort me with calming words: "You're young. You can handle this. You will be okay."

I lay down, closing my eyes. As the tears roll down my face, she infuses the Benadryl. That was OK. Now it was time to inject the chemo. I calmed myself as much as possible. I put myself into a deep meditative state. "Okay, we're starting," the nurse said.

I begin to recite the same prayer over and over as I felt the poison entering my body. It felt like molten liquid rushing through my veins, slowly creeping up my arm, through my chest and spreading across my body until it invaded my feet. Rather than fight it, I decide to make friends with "Chemo". Chemo would become my ally in this war. Together we would kill the enemy that had invaded my body.

I envisioned the light that would destroy the cancer. The Benadryl made me drowsy, lulling me into a sleep. Then from a distance, I heard: "Mrs. Kontos it's over." I opened my eyes. *I did well*, I thought, *I'm okay. Thank you, Lord.*

Despite feeling weak and drowsy, I walked to the car by myself. Not sure how I didn't fall, but that was my fight. I slumped into the passenger seat for the drive home and lost track of time and motion. I didn't know where I was. I felt so drugged... all I could hear was the driver screaming at me. It was noise that overwhelmed my mind. I ignored it. I got home and passed out.

When I awoke and realized that I had survived the first chemotherapy treatment, I felt good, knowing that I had found my inner lioness who could battle ferociously. *Okay*, I thought: *Let's do this, it's on!* Someone was going to come out alive, and that someone was going to be me!

Walking the Line

Before chemo, my hair was long with beautiful strawberry blond streaks. Within two weeks of the treatment starting, I was beginning to lose all that. I did not want to see myself looking sick and I knew I did not want to have others see me with pity in their eyes. I hate pity. I hated being looked at like death had come over me. It made me feel as though my energy had been sapped; I needed only positive energy.

I decided to buy a wig. That was something I could control, and I did. There are so many different types. I saw prices ranging from $50 to $3,500. From crappy synthetics to amazing real hair. I visited a few stores and tried many different wigs. My friend, who is an amazing hairdresser, came for the ride. I even had Nikki help me choose. It was important to me that Nikki feel she was doing something to help me during this time.

So, of course, I had to try the Marilyn (Monroe) wig. I have to admit I looked darn good as Marilyn. I even wore the bright red lipstick and sang Happy Birthday Mr. President. Next, I tried the flamboyant red Latino look. And then the layered 80s, the I'm-a-rock -star look and the blond bob *Pulp Fiction* look.

On and on, we tried them all, taking pictures and laughing, forgetting ourselves for a little while. In the end, I chose an expensive real hair wig from Europe. It was long, over my shoulders: a natural sandy blond. My hairdresser cut, streaked and styled it to my liking. I have to admit, it was quite beautiful. In fact, people would stop me to ask who did my hair. Very amusing.

There was no escaping the fact that my hair was going to fall out, so I cut my hair a couple of times to get ready for the inevitable. About a week into chemo, my hair started falling on my face. It was emotionally traumatic: I did not want to wake up and find a clump of hair on my pillow. It was time: wearing a white camisole, I took my place in front of the mirror that covered the entire bathroom wall and with an electric shaver in one hand, I shaved it all off, strip by strip. I pictured myself as Demi Moore in *GI Jane*. Fierce and fearlessly, I looked at the clumping hair eager to fall from my scalp, a symbol of my cancer falling away.

As the hair dropped to the floor, I felt brave and powerful. Cancer was falling off my head. I had slain it. I had killed it. I was a warrior. *Fuck YOU Cancer!*

Chapter Seven

The Secret

When you place humility over your ego, you experience growth. Having an open mind and heart to everything that comes your way makes you a leader and a well-rounded, emotionally intelligent individual. It opens you up to the world and experiences that ignorance blocks

– Catherine Kontos

Stripped Bare

In Buddhist philosophy, there is the belief that to find oneself, one must first strip away the ego. The ego consists of identities we latch onto for the sake of vanity, socialization, materialism, and the "true" self: our authentic core. It is all that transcends the limitations of the earthly body.

Nothing strips your ego more than having cancer. Scarred and bald, no eyebrows or lashes: all that I identified with my womanhood, femininity, beauty, sensuality, and sexuality were now gone – forever. My ego didn't know what to do with me. Who was I now? I couldn't stand catching my reflection in the mirror. A huge part of how I presented myself to the world was in my stride and my pride. Catherine with the long blonde hair. Catherine with the almond-shaped eyes and long lashes. Catherine, so radiant and vibrantly healthy. Where had she gone? I looked so ill, and yet I would not allow how I looked to interfere with my fight to get healthy again. I would not give in or give up.

I accepted that I had to isolate myself for protection and that planning for anything would be difficult. As I looked through social media, I watched as people carried on with their lives: attending events, getting married, taking vacations. All I could think was that my life would be on hold for the next year, which was the hardest aspect for me at that time. Social interaction had always been my coping strategy, but I couldn't use it now to deal with my cancer battle and all the issues I had.

There was no way around it. I had to face everything head-on as it came. No running away. I was not only battling cancer; I was also confronting my demons. Would I break?

I went into isolation with my cancer and every question I ever had about my existence. Solitary confinement, almost like a Buddhist monk. The retreat that I had sought out at the beginning of my journey was forced on me now. Only it wasn't exotic, distant, or Zen-like with candles and incense burning. It was my four walls: me and my bed.

At first, I was extremely uncomfortable being alone so much, but then I began to wonder whether it was really a loss, or perhaps a gift? I kept close anyone or anything that was positive and uplifting. As for the rest, I made sure to limit my exposure. I stayed in my room for the worst parts of my journey – no TV or radio. I wanted to control what my mind was fed. I only streamed movies or shows that would boost my mood and lift me. News was off-limits. I figured I would learn about anything "urgent" eventually. This is what I still practice today. I remember during one point at the end of my therapies, *ISIS* – the terrorist group – was reaping havoc on the world, and I was clueless. Was being clueless a good thing or bad? Not sure.

Every morning I meditated with guided imagery. I found videos that helped me envision eradicating cancer from my body and being healthy once again. At night I would fall asleep either with earphones listening to prayers or through guided sleep meditation. During the day, I devoured motivational videos. I stayed away from people who caused me to feel negative emotions. Unfortunately, this could not always be avoided. So I holed up in my room, the only place I felt safe. I refused to have my emotions influenced by others' aggression, fears, and worries. All I wanted was to feel love and a sense of security, which I got from those I allowed in my space.

Alone time started to feel a lot less frightening. It was a cleanse, detoxing from noise, news and negativity. I selected carefully what I allowed in. It was a rebirth, and I started to like it.

I had told doctors and nurses right from the first meeting that I did not want them to share statistics unless I asked. Nor did I want to know the rare, long-term effects of my therapies. Why did I need to know any of this? I chose to do chemotherapy, and, yes, I was aware there were side effects that could make me sick, or even kill me. But why feed my mind with possible negative effects? To feel fear, develop psychosomatic symptoms? Every little pain or sensation, I would think, *Oh, it's this, or Oh it's that…* Absolutely not! If something came up, I would address it with the doctor, and I would deal with it then.

This was my fight, and I was doing it on my terms. I had never been more certain of anything in my life. I had one thing to do: beat this. I believed right down to my core that I would. Although my fight was with cancer, I was also battling to keep my mind from being trapped by the tentacles of fear.

If I felt fear, I would acknowledge its presence and source – then let it go. Being fearless does not mean never feeling fear; it means not letting it take over your mind and paralyze you. You have to kick its butt to the curb; not let it steer you in a direction that prevents you from making decisions needed for a better life. A life filled with hope, not fear.

Stoned

As I reached the two-week mark since my chemotherapy treatment, I still didn't know how sick I was, neither did the doctors. I felt good, considering what I had been through. My hair was gone, but I felt physically well. Suddenly a sharp pain hit the left side of my back. It's back... *Oh Dear Lord... it's back!*

The kidney stone pain that had been in remission came back with a vengeance. This was bad timing... or was it? I rushed to the ER. I knew the two-week mark was when I was supposed to be most vulnerable to infection. But since it was my first chemotherapy session, it was expected that my blood would still be stable. My doctors had not even planned blood tests.

The Emergency Room was full. I wore a mask as a precautionary measure, and they placed me in an open corner cubicle with curtains. They ran blood tests (my forearm turned black-and-blue from their attempts to find a vein) and took a scan. The results confirmed that I had a 9.5 mm stone stuck in the tube between my kidney and bladder. The blood tests also revealed I was neutropenic, meaning my white blood cell count was down to almost zero.

The doctors were in a panic. This isn't supposed to happen after the first chemotherapy treatment, especially to a strong 40-year-old. But I wasn't that surprised. I had warned them about the interaction of drugs with my body. Now they believed me. My fear was coming true. This was a dangerous combination, and it was about to get worse during the next week.

Doctors told me they needed to insert a tube to allow my urine to bypass the stone so as not to risk infection and kidney failure. Even inserting the tube presented a risk of infection. Within minutes, they had given me an elevated dose of antibiotics intravenously and continued injecting my stomach area to increase my white blood cell count. They brought me to a room with about six staffers, including medical students, who watched a screen showing images from the camera that had been inserted with the tube. I looked at the camera and jokingly said to one of the medical students:

"I feel like I'm in an episode of *Grey's Anatomy*. Look at all of you – you look like movie stars. Which one of you is McDreamy and who's McSteamy?"

They all started laughing. Well, I figured if this was my time, I might as well go out with laughter. Again, what choice did I have? None. Should I have cried? I needed to make the best of it. Needless to say, being sedated did help!

I remained in the ER for four days as they continued observing and injecting me. It was not comforting to discover that there was a patient with tuberculosis in isolation nearby. I wanted to leave, hoping that the stone would come out on its own.

A few days after I was released, I felt pain in my left arm and noticed a large reddish lump on the side of my elbow. It hurt to touch. I noted the time: 4 p.m. I called my nurse and told her I might have a blood clot forming in my arm. I described to her exactly what was happening. She said: "Come immediately to the hospital. I'll have an ultrasound ready for you, and, hopefully, you get to see the doctor before he leaves. I'll have him wait for you as long as he can."

It was rush hour: was I going to make it? Why were these complications happening to me? I arrived at the hospital just in time. The ultrasound and the doctor confirmed it was a type of blood clot called a "deep vein thrombosis". A blood clot, if left untreated can migrate to the lungs where it can create a fatal pulmonary embolism. The doctor gave me a prescription to inject my abdomen with blood thinners twice a day, for the next three months.

> *Only the light seen in the dark will give you the push for hope and change.*
>
> **– Catherine Kontos**

I had planned my daughter's birthday party for one week later, intentionally scheduling it before my next chemotherapy treatment. Nothing would get in the way of my making it epic: it had to be memorable because I knew tomorrow, was never promised. We reserved for that Sunday afternoon a nightclub with a stage and big screens which were to play music videos with an 80s theme. There was going to be a fashion show where the kids would display their cool outfits, a dance competition and a Pac-Man cake for dessert. Of course, I was to be the MC.

I remember arriving at the venue feeling beyond exhausted and weak. I did not know how I was going to get through the next few hours. I sat in the car as it was unloaded. I thought to myself: *Okay, you can do this... you have to do this*. I got out of the car: it was showtime. There was no way I was going to look sick or tired. Not that day.

Ever heard the expression: "energy is contagious"? Well, that's what happened. The kids were so excited: there was a barman serving non-alcoholic Shirley Temple drinks all afternoon; food was abundant and, of course, lots of candy. Seeing Nikki and her friends having the time of their lives infused me with energy. I did not sit the entire time. I even danced a little. The kids strutted their stuff in the fashion show. Nikki was elated: it was a huge success. But as I stood there leaning against a pole, I felt my energy waning. I finally asked my cousin for a chair.

December 13th, 2013

Got dizzy in shower. Ate. Still dizzy. Got lightheaded. Recovered after lunch. We went out for dinner 'til midnight.

December 14th, 2013

Felt extreme fatigue and weakness, dizziness, very lightheaded, pains all over like I'm 100 years old, pain to the touch. Felt so weak, like I'm anemic. Loss of appetite. Could barely make sentences.

A couple of days later, it was time for my second chemotherapy treatment. My count was back up, thanks to the medication. Everything seemed stable. Fast-forward two weeks and it was Christmas time. I woke up feeling tired, but I dressed, put on my wig, and makeup and went outside to clean the snow and ice off my car. I drove myself to the hospital with my mom to take my weekly blood tests. As I waited, the nurse asked how I was feeling. "Tired, but good," I replied. "I have to finish my Christmas shopping and go grocery shopping."

My nurse was a woman in her 50s with strong facial features – a poker face of sorts. Blonde, thin and tall. I often wondered how these nurses summoned the strength to help cancer patients on a daily basis. How is it they don't break? As I awaited my results, I was laughing with my mom and discussing what I should buy my mother-in-law for Christmas. I looked up and saw the nurse coming towards me. I knew from the look in her eyes that she did not have good news.

"What were your plans today?" she asked. "I'm going shopping for Christmas," I replied. It was the 23ʳᵈ of December, and I needed to make sure I did this. She looked at me as she pulled out her chart with my blood test results. She pointed at the numbers. My white blood cell count had dropped almost to zero again. She said:

"I'm sorry you need to go straight home."

She gave me a mask, a box of pills, and a prescription for neutropenia injections. She said: "Catherine, the clinic is closed the next few days for Christmas. You will likely get a fever. If so, take these pills right away and rush to the emergency."

She gave me enough injections for my neutropenia to last for 11 days. This was the maximum dose; in all her years as a nurse, she had never seen the maximum dose prescribed, not even in patients twice my age. On top of that, I still had the tube in me for the kidney stone that was lingering, plus a blood clot. I had now been upgraded as having a high risk of dying, and I knew it. I wore the mask. My mom, oblivious to what was going on asked: "What's happening?" *(Τι γίνετε;)*

Not wanting to scare her, I replied: "Mom, they are just being cautious. They want me to wear the mask. Now let's go shopping. We have things to do." *(Μαμά, είναι απλός προληπτικό. Θέλουν να φορέσω τη μάσκα. Πάμε για ψώνια. Έχουμε πράγματα να κάνουμε.)*

I went shopping for Christmas gifts with my mask on and bought my mother-in-law a beautiful winter coat. We then went grocery shopping. I did not touch a thing; my mother picked the groceries, pushed the cart and opened the doors. She was my angel on earth, my saving grace. I don't know what I would have done without her. All this took about an hour. By the time we were done, I felt that my fatigue level had increased 10-fold. The 15-minute drive home felt like an hour. I collapsed on my bed.

Faith over Fear

It was Christmas. I did not want to burden my family with how sick I felt. So I fudged the truth and told them that my blood counts were a little low and that I needed to rest in bed with my mask on.

It was a tradition to always have Christmas dinner at my home, but that had to change for obvious reasons. This year, Christmas dinner would be at my brother's. I lay under a white duvet in my king-sized, mahogany sleigh bed praying continuously from morning to night in my darkened room, where the only light even during the daytime was a thin quiver peeking through the strips of the vertical blinds. It felt like a trance. When I closed my eyes, I felt calm and meditative as though I could feel my soul. Every breath was mindful; every thought was focused on recovery. In those moments, I felt no fear and even accepted death as my possible fate.

That was key: I had to stare death in the face and accept it. Fearing it would only make me think of it more. I no longer allowed it in my headspace or in my heart. There was no room for it; it would no longer control my decisions, my life. I needed to feel in my gut, heart, and deepest inner being that I would beat cancer, that I would live well into my 80s. Truly believe it; not fake believe it – and I did. I became focused, like an athlete in the zone – tunnel vision. Nothing else mattered, but my fight against the beast. Fear had finally lost its power over me.

I remained in this state for two days. I prayed, and I asked Him: "Please Lord, spare me from a fever. Please, I don't want to end up in the hospital for Christmas. My family... I can't do this to them, especially not to my little girl."

I repeated my prayers and request over and over. Christmas

morning came, and my wish had been granted. No fever. My fatigue was overwhelming, and although risky, I gathered my strength and decided I would go to the Christmas dinner – an enjoyable couple of hours – then come home. I went to my brother's, took off my mask for a couple of hours, and made the Christmas dinner as normal as possible. It was exactly what I needed. Afterward, I went home, collapsed on my bed and slept with a smile on my face and a heart filled with gratitude.

Two days later, I got a call from my nurse. She asked, "How are you? How was your Christmas?" I replied: "It went well, considering everything." She replied with surprise: "I was expecting your name to appear on the Emergency Room list. I was shocked not to see your name. I was certain that you would have been there in your condition. How did you not end up there?"

My answer: "With a whole lot of praying, God granted me my wish. My temperature never rose, not even a little. I thank God for that because He spared me and granted my wish to be with my family at Christmas."

It was a miracle. My Christmas miracle.

December 28th, 2013

I sit here crying cuz I'm stuck in a marriage and I'm miserable. I'm stuck cuz if I leave, I will break up a family. I will hurt so many people.

People think I'm happy. Weird is that I am, despite everything. I know how to be happy away from all that. But I feel stuck. I want to be free. To live. Why can't I forgive?

New Year's Eve came, and I remember staying up to watch the ball drop as everyone else slept. I didn't know if it would be my last one. I woke up Nikki, who was lying on my lap, right before midnight to make sure we brought the New Year in together. As I hugged her, I closed my eyes, cherishing that moment. I thought about future joys with my daughter that cancer threatened: *Would I be there to have her tell me about her first kiss? Would I be there to wipe her tears when he broke her heart? Would I celebrate her Sweet Sixteen? Would I see her graduate and get married?*

Even though I believed I would make it, the reality is that we all die eventually. Although I had convinced myself I would not die, I also could not deny that the Grim Reaper was looming nearby, waiting for an opportunity to collect my soul. I just needed to make sure never to open that door. So the question is, how long do we have? What imprint and what legacy will we leave behind? How will people know I even existed? These were the questions that shaped me into the person I am today. My every moment, my every move since must be purposeful. Be it small or big, I move ahead hoping I make a difference and that the life gifted to me is not wasted.

January 6th, 2014

I feel like a wounded soldier in a war full of obvious scars screaming loudly at me. Getting up after every battle and fighting again. I feel fire burning through my veins, brain and blood. I feel it right through my skin. I feel broken. How can I be sexy or attractive? Emotionally I'm lost. My mind hurts from all the pain. My baby cries herself to sleep worrying about me, missing me. How is this fair to her?

I need to make big decisions. I distract myself too much. I worked six hours today. I feel this need to be alone. Denial, escape is creeping in. No denying it anymore. The scars are in my face. Bald head; hair grows, but scars are there forever! Tonight, I'm sad, very sad. I've got to change my frame of mind.

January 7th, 2014

Had an emotional breakdown last night. Mostly thinking of my scars. It took a couple of hours. Barely slept. I only can think about how no one will want me all scarred. I feel like I'm stuck. I can't leave. Who would want someone who is scarred, has had cancer? I feel damaged. I feel like I have to end it and I'm resisting. Why? I'm so tired of tormenting myself. Can I ever love him again? Can I ever forgive him? I need to be loved. I deserve to be loved. But how do I do this without losing everything? I need space from everyone and everything. I need time alone.

January 8th, 2014

Woke up often. Became extremely light-headed. Felt very anxious and depressed throughout day. Almost fainted. Light-headed, anxiety, hot. No appetite in the evening.

Why should I live miserably? Life's short. I feel so alone. I need to be alone. I need to figure it all out.

January 10th, 2014

Stayed in bed all day depressed.

By the 11th straight day of solitude and isolation, my schedule started to feel well... routine. Meditate. Pray. Inject my abdomen twice daily. One medication to increase my white blood cells and a second injection with the blood thinners. I would do this morning and night. I had become an expert. Every inch of my abdomen had been pierced with a needle. Each time I had to go one inch over or under to inject. My abs were full of hard lumps and bruised. A couple of times, the needles broke while injecting. Overall, I became pretty good at something I wish I never needed to learn.

> *Blessed is one that has friends that are as clear as water. Surround yourself with wings.*
>
> **– Catherine Kontos**

Being alone was one thing, but by now I was starting to feel lonely. I needed to see people and socialize. I definitely started to feel like it was time to leave these four walls. So for a change of scenery, I took a drive – a drive with no destination in the winter cold. I could not be in public due to the risk of catching the flu or a virus. A hug, kiss, or touch was forbidden. I started taking drives often, but it was never enough. It felt like I was inside a television watching from the inside out: people walking into stores to shop; some taking buses, others walking or driving to their destinations. I watched through restaurant windows as other families and their friends had dinner. I wasn't part of anything and lived solely on what I saw on my drives and in social media.

It was a loneliness I had never experienced, one only another cancer fighter could understand. No matter how much support you have, you are alone in this fight – both physically and mentally. You either give up or you rise to the biggest challenge of your life.

By luck, I reunited with my elementary school friends on social media. They started posting pictures of us as children, and we communicated via those posts and group chats. I was so grateful to reconnect with what felt like long-lost family. The laughter and social interaction brought some comfort. Initially, none of them knew I was sick; I started reaching out to as many as I could find. It was an exciting distraction for all of us, meeting again after 28 years. I wondered about the coincidence of these friends coming back into my life at a time that I most needed them.

These friends were like brothers and sisters to me, most of us growing up in the Park Extension where first-generation Greek immigrants usually raised their families. It is a small area of Montreal with one of the most condensed populations made up of low-income families struggling to make ends meet. A long fence and bushes separate it from one of the wealthiest municipalities in Montreal called Town of Mount Royal. As children, we would look at this fence saying, "One day I will live on the other side of the fence."

Our parents, like most immigrants, came to Canada with only a suitcase and hopes of a better life. They made sure that there was food on the table and that we were educated. Some built empires out of that suitcase and the sheer will to provide a better life for their children. Others not so much. But we all lived with strong family values. Although financially limited in my youth, my parents saved and managed to place me in a Greek private school, as did my friends' families. Our parents embedded our culture in us: whether at home or school, the values were the same. Families and teachers were very strict with respect being priority No. 1.

To this day, I know that the re-emergence of my childhood friends at that time in my life gave me the positive emotional energy I needed to fight cancer. Part of me even thought that perhaps this joy was a gift from God: you know how they say, your life flashes before your eyes before you die? Maybe this was God's way to help me say goodbye to everyone in my life. I can say now that it was not that: it was simply a gift of love.

For most of Christmas, New Year's Day and my 41st birthday, I was sick in bed. The chemotherapy "bombs" were strong. On most days, I was grateful to be able to open my eyes and have another chance to fight. At one point, everyone in my house was sick with colds, and I had to stay completely isolated from them. My mom was careful about how she prepared my food. She was sick as well. Even in isolation, my mask was on. I remember at one point my daughter was at my bedroom door peeking in at me in bed. She knew she wasn't allowed in. She stood there staring at me with her mask on, and I looked at her as I spoke through my mask, telling her how much I loved her. She cried. I knew she needed to hold me. I looked at her as she sobbed by the doorway, telling me how much she missed me. I still can't explain how I knew, but I just knew that when this was all over, I would be OK.

Nothing was more important to me than holding my child and comforting her. I looked at her and told her, "Baby come here." She cried, "No mommy, I don't want to hurt you and make you sicker." I said, "Mommy needs a hug to feel better." She came running in and we fell into each other's arms, crying and smiling at the same time. "Mommy needed that more than medicine. You just made mommy better."

She left my room with a smile that resonated through her body and mine. Love is very powerful. It changes the chemistry in your body and can help you fight a dreaded disease. The deep outpouring of love from everyone filled my soul, helping me fight the beast.

Birthing Me

After two weeks of isolation, I was finally released from what I considered my time of reflection and rebirth. Now I had to get ready to blow up my kidney stones. Remember those painful buggers? They were still in me, adding to my litany of woes: cancer with accompanying dreadful chemotherapy treatments;   potentially life-threatening blood clots; blood counts so low that even a minute amount of bacteria in my body could turn into a fatal infection; and, last but not least, the stubborn stones and the tube that had been inserted in me and could itself cause an infection.

Since the stone refused to come out, I would now have to add a procedure whereby they would attempt to blow up the stone using sonar waves. Did I mention that this procedure could also blow up nearby veins and cause internal bleeding? It felt as though my body was out to kill me. Like any other cancer patient, I was told not to shave, and not to have pedicures or manicures. I was supposed to wear gloves while performing any activity because even a small cut could put me at risk of infection. Yet, I was going to undergo voluntarily a procedure that could destroy my veins and cause internal bleeding. I say "voluntarily", but I really had no choice. So once again, I had to accept my possible death. I stopped feeling fear. It was strange; I felt deathly calm (excuse the pun). This was a time in my life when I should have been most fearful, yet facing death in the eye and surrendering to pure faith was the best gift I had been given during this time. I had alchemized fear into faith. I was riding faith's tail. I completely surrendered and trusted in my faith, even if it might mean my death. It was a freedom I had never experienced.

The doctors wanted my blood counts to be at their highest levels before putting me through the procedure. After 11 days of injecting myself with neutropenia, not only did my blood counts go up, they were abundantly higher than normal. Obviously, this was not what the doctors wanted. They were left with their mouths agape as to how my body had, once again, hyper-reacted to a drug. Supposedly my blood count being higher than normal was not dangerous for me. I can tell you that I sure was energized, the best I had felt in months.

In the following days, I was given antibiotics as a preventive measure. The procedure went as expected, but, unfortunately, it did not work. The stone did not shatter. Instead I voided blood from all the veins that had blown up. Laser surgery was my last option to burst the stone. Yet another challenge. Why was I not surprised? But I never lost my focus; I knew I was going to be fine and that once I got through the fire, I would be reborn.

Again, everything was coordinated with the doctors. I approached the secretary and asked her for an appointment. She told me, "The doctor usually does this procedure on Wednesdays, but on the week you will be operated, he's exceptionally coming in on Tuesday." She filled out the appointment paper and gave it to me. I smiled when I saw the date was the 22nd. "*It's on the 22nd. My dad's got my back. I'll be fine.*"

As I left the hospital, I felt peace and serenity, knowing without a doubt that my guardian angel had sent me a message. He's with me. Always.

I started pumping myself with drugs to prepare for the kidney stone treatment. The timing was interesting, as well, because I was also about to undergo the last of the chemotherapy bombs before switching to a new chemotherapy drug, which I was looking forward to because the last ones had almost killed me.

The treatment to break up the stone that had tormented me for six months was a success. It was shattered to bits, and the tube was finally removed. I was out of the danger zone. One by one, everything had its ending. Kidney stone gone, chemotherapy bombs finished, neutropenia no more, and blood clot taken care of.

Life is not all good or all bad. Like everything in life, there are beginnings and there are endings; one should never lose hope during the bad times. The sun is hiding behind every dark cloud, and it will shine through eventually. It's inevitable. Always be grateful for the good times. Life always throws curveballs to challenge you, over and over. Expect the unexpected and remember that these challenges are there to teach you and help you grow, no matter how uncomfortable they may be. Life is interesting that way.

Chapter Eight

Flickering Light

When we like or love someone, we often make excuses for their bad behavior: by doing so, we are training them to mistreat us. Then one day the rose-colored glasses come off, and you realize that you don't even recognize them anymore. The truth is they always showed you who they were. You just didn't want to see it because it fit with the image you needed them to be at the time.

– Catherine Kontos

Blackout

As I began my new chemotherapy drug, I also realized a new kind of reality: a good one actually. I had no side effects whatsoever. If anything, I felt good. I would get up, dress, and go to my weekly chemotherapy treatment with a smile, knowing I was in the last half of my journey. At one point, my hair even started growing back. I went to the doctor pulled off my wig and pointed at my head and asked: "Doctor is this normal?" He looked at me with disbelief: "No. Are you having any of the other side effects?" I answered, "No, nothing. Is the chemo working?" I asked amusingly. "I'm sure it is... well it's all good," he said. "I think you have been through enough."

Spring had just sprung, and for the first time in what felt like forever, I came alive – going out with friends and family. Everything was looking up, except my marriage. At home, things had taken a turn for the worst. The final tornado of what I thought was a whirlwind of a life had descended. My marriage ended in the early spring, while I was in chemotherapy. So many years, so much invested, all just a memory now, I was suddenly, not only battling cancer, not only attempting a new business, but I was a single mom doing it all. It was just me and my daughter now; a two-girl team. A team where she had to grow up fast and I had to support her emotionally through another huge change in her life. A team where my recovery and her well-being needed to be equally important.

Because without my daughter, I couldn't care about anything else, and without my health, I was no good to anyone, especially my daughter. She needed me more than ever. By this point, she was 11 and had become a scared little girl, filled with anxiety. I didn't realize how affected she was until one day she unwittingly let me in on it. I had noticed that she had become very clingy. More than usual. My eyes and ears opened to her actual thoughts when I noticed she would ask me every single night: "Mommy, did you lock the door?" "Did you put the alarm on?" "Mommy, are you sure?"

I thought that with everything happening this was normal behavior of a child feeling unsettled. I was wrong.

It was a beautiful sunny spring day, and we were driving with the top down and the sun shining on our heads. All was normal, or so I thought. I noticed Nikki had become very quiet. I glanced over at her every once in a while. We stopped at a red light, and I asked her: "Baby, what's wrong? Is something wrong?"

Suddenly she burst into big, fat tears and the words were barely coherent. "Mommy I'm scared. I'm scared someone will come, take you or hurt you. I don't want you to die."

My heart jumped into my throat in that moment, realizing how fragile and imaginative a child's mind could be. She told me something that she had seen and heard, and it scared her to the point that she created a whole story in her head.

I calmed her down and reassured her that the fears were not warranted. She was living in fear more than I had thought. I did not realize how a child could translate a situation so differently than an adult. I knew at that moment that communication with her needed to be very clear because her imagination was creating havoc in her mind. I knew now never to assume what she was experiencing and thinking. I knew that from then on, I needed to ask her about her thoughts and feelings.

Life had been very unfair to her. She had seen and experienced things that no child should witness. She was in a lot of pain. Even though most of it was out my control, I placed all the burden on myself. No matter how sick or weak I felt, I did everything a kid needs a mom to do. I got up, drove her to school in my pajamas, and stayed in the car watching her walk into school. I brought her to karate, to the doctor, to her friends' houses. I took out the garbage, did the laundry, made the beds. There was always fresh food in the fridge and hot meals to eat. I wanted her to feel safe, loved and taken care of, so she'd know that we were going to get through it. Together – as a team.

She needed less disruption in her life and time to heal from her own anxiety and fears. An earthquake had just shaken both our souls, and we were struggling. How was I going to do this alone now? I was running on fumes. Would we end up on the street? Would I be able to handle the stress of a divorce and not get sicker? I didn't know where or how we'd end up, but I knew I had to show up for Nikki in every way possible.

Beyond the cancer, I needed to be a mother who was present, an entrepreneur in a new struggling business, and a property manager. At the time, a government tax audit loomed over my head, as well as lawsuits, and a very challenging divorce. I didn't have time to think about cancer. I was too busy putting out fires. Life was chasing me, and so were the flames. Any person would have broken. My sadness was to the point where all my nurses noticed. The cancer patient who used to dress for chemotherapy sessions like she was going to a dinner party was now showing up without makeup, wearing sweatpants. This woman who had flirted with death had reached her wits' end. That woman was me. I desperately needed to grasp someone's hand for help. I remember walking into my nurse's office one desperate day; she looked up at me and her face dropped. The first words that fell from my mouth were: "Please get me help. I need help."

I was placed with a psychologist and red-flagged for suicide. My flame had burnt out. I went into therapy twice a week; within three weeks, I was feeling better, stronger. That's all it took for me to get over that hump. I was still sad, but I was able to brush myself off and focus once again. Divorce is not fun. Divorce while fighting cancer is a lot less fun. We got matters settled within weeks, and by the time I had started my radiation, it was a done deal. Fighting for my life was priority No. 1, so I settled with whatever it took to end it quickly. I had to choose my wars, and I chose to fight for my life, to focus everything on it. One by one, I took care of each issue.

I remember one morning I was putting on my makeup when my lawyer called. She told me that after three years, the government had decided to close my file. The audit that would have forced me into bankruptcy was now over. I broke down crying with relief. The lawyer's voice cracked as she congratulated me. I just kept thanking her. She didn't know how much that call saved me. She had no idea that I was sick. She only heard my voice over the phone throughout that time. The rest of the lawsuits came and went.

Everything slowly subsided as new challenges came. I realized how we are always looking to find a moment in our lives where we have surpassed all challenges, and life is smooth. That is so unrealistic.

The minute you surpass one obstacle, another arrives; that is if you are lucky. Like the well-known expression goes: When it rains, it pours. This expectation of relieving yourself of all obstacles is where misery resides. When you understand that you already have everything, that is when you will be happy in life. That is called gratitude. Once you change your perspective from, "I don't have enough" to "I already have everything I need", life just feels better. Challenges become a part of life, and you surpass them a lot easier and quicker. When in misery, you focus on your problems more than your blessings. When you do so, your every move and thought pull you toward a negative outcome. You end up living in this whirlwind world of survival and dissatisfaction that no one but you can do anything about.

Change your perspective. Change your life.

I could have easily given up. I had every reason to. I woke up every day with a heavy heart and severe anxiety, trying to catch my breath. But it never stopped me from showing up as every person I needed to be in order to get through the next hour, the next day. Yes, I lived to survive by the hour at times, and on good days, I was able to look at surviving the day. I could not look beyond a day. It was too overwhelming. So, every day, I would wake up and the first thing I'd say upon opening my two eyes was: "Thank you. Thank you for letting me live another day. Thank you for keeping me and my family safe. Thank you for giving me strength."

The list never ended. I talked to Him daily and thanked Him for everything I had to live for. He knew when I was mad at Him, and He knew when I was frustrated. I would ask Him for help all the time. I prayed to Him, and no matter how bad things were, I put my faith in Him – even if I wasn't happy about my present journey. I trusted the journey and knew that I would make it to the other side in health and joy.

The other behavior I incorporated into my daily routine was listening to motivational videos. Next were my morning and nightly meditations. Every one of these behaviors was to insulate my mind from for all the noise. I not only needed to stay sane but to be on my game. I would go to my oncology psychologist and talk to her about everything except my cancer. She was concerned that I never spoke about cancer. My response to her was as follows: "I know I have cancer. I'm not in denial, nor am I avoiding it. There's nothing I can do more than what I already do. I have no control over it. Whether I live or die, it's not up to me. So why worry about it?"

I would ask her: "Are you trying to depress me?" She looked at me with concern: "No, but I am worried that one day it will all hit you and you will break." I replied; "We'll see."

Summer came and I found myself slowly making my way back to a semi-normal life. My wig in stifling hot, humid weather felt like a Russian fur hat, but I got through it.

I disguised my missing eyebrows and lashes with makeup. I dressed up and at my elementary school reunion a couple of weeks after my last chemotherapy session – still fatigued and swollen from months of brutal treatments, I danced and drank just like everyone else. How wonderful is that?

Was I really still here or was I dreaming? We had reunited to celebrate our childhood friendships, but I also came to celebrate life. I was alive and I felt free. Truly a night I will never forget. I was euphoric because for the first time that I could remember, none of my struggles weighed on me. At least for that night.

Everything was slowly fixing itself, but my fight was not over yet. Soon after the reunion, my radiation treatment was in full swing: 29 visits that lasted through August.

At the end of my radiation treatments, I decided to take Nikki on a two-week road trip to Maine. We packed our bags and drove south, just me and my sweet girl to what was a perfect celebration for the tough year we had passed. A celebration marking where my journey as a fighter ended and my journey as a survivor began.

With every mile we drove along the highway, I had the feeling that every one of my problems was disappearing. Our combined excitement was infectious. We were giggling, laughing, dancing in our seats, singing at the top of our lungs – not a care in the world. It was pure silliness and uncaged abandon.

Being by the water had always been my solace and my muse. In sadness, I would go there to think; and in joy, I would be inspired. I remember my first time taking Ogunquit's scenic coastal walk known as the Marginal Way, knowing that I was exactly where I needed to be. The tide was up: waves hitting rocks, a refreshing salty breeze and endless sky on the horizon! This was the medicine both Nikki and I needed. The lobster rolls were definitely a happy bonus. I reflected on everything with a lingering sadness, still grieving all the losses. For the first time, I was able to think about and absorb all I had just passed. My losses ran deep, but so too did my treasures. Everything we lose and everything we have is the tapestry of our lives, and we have to work with the challenges and treasures that we're given to weave a life we love, one of meaning and purpose. There are lessons in every thread.

My hope for a better life was in the forefront of my thoughts. A life free from sickness. Free of toxicity. Free from legal battles. I knew from this day forward as I worked on my cleanup that I would also attract exactly the right energy needed to bring peace and harmony to my life. No amount of money and no other person other than I could ensure that. This time with Nikki – away from the mess that we were leaving behind for two weeks – I found peace again. I needed the time to calm my soul from the trauma it had been through. As strong as I was, I knew that I was fragile, both mentally and physically. It had been a hell of a year.

AfterShock

As the dust began to settle, I finally felt that I could move forward. I was not who I was before my world came crashing down on me. In some ways, I felt mentally stronger and in other ways weaker. The brain fog or chemo brain was not helping. People often have a hard time finding work that will accommodate their doctor appointments. When they do go back to work – if they are strong enough to go back to work – everything is harder. The year or two of not working adds a financial burden to the already extremely stressful circumstances of being sick. I had so many appointments that I was able to work only part-time. When I did work, I worked at a fast pace to make up for the lost time, which left me exhausted. I was living the life of a survivor.

Physically I had changed forever. I didn't look the same. It felt like I had invaded someone else's body. I got all kinds of unfamiliar aches and numbness out of nowhere. My hair was growing sporadically; it felt weird and looked like an SOS pad. I was not as strong as I was before, and I fatigued early on every day. I was out of shape. Before starting chemo, I had decided to gain five pounds on purpose, thinking I would throw up and lose a lot of weight once I started my treatments. To my surprise, I was wrong. The steroids they give you during treatment make you gain weight. Now 20 pounds heavier and my treatments in the past, I kept gaining weight.

Fall came roaring in a riot of leafy color, and my social life bloomed again. I started going out and making up for time that had been lost while I was locked in. That, of course, came with consequences: I gained another 40 pounds. Chemo had really slowed down my metabolism and it was showing. My attempts to work out at the gym were not successful, nor was there much success with my diets. So the weight just piled up. Then I noticed my arm swelling. I was diagnosed with lymphedema, a lifelong after-effect that caused my arm to swell after 14 lymph nodes were removed and the remaining few were radiated.

Most people think that when cancer is over that the cancer survivors are doing well because they look well. The reality is that they are dealing with a lot of the stresses from the aftermath of being sick. They are often dealing with it alone. I was struggling: tired much of the time and very little energy. But somehow, I would find enough to do everything I needed to…until I broke, once again.

It was January. Nights were really long and the days were freezing cold. I suddenly woke up in the middle of the night and – boom – it hit me. She told me it would… I started having flashbacks about everything I had experienced. One memory after the other flooded my mind. I began to cry and all I kept uttering was: "I was left to die. I was left to die. I was left to die." The words I was told 16 months earlier resonated in my mind, *Just die already…*

Anger, sadness and fear overcame me. The trifecta to perfect misery. Let me start with my anger. I became bitter. The anger was just eating away at me, bit by bit. I was angry I got cancer. I was angry that I lost my business. I was angry that I was divorced. I was angry at the world. I was angry for being placed in a position where I was struggling so much. I felt alone and betrayed. In the end, when you close the door to your home, you are on your own.

Nobody can understand your struggles or your pain, not even if you tell them; these people are not inside your head with you. Even when they know, there's only so much they can do. The rest of the time, you are alone. There's a saying: "You come in this world alone. You die alone." That's how I felt. Even with all the help I did get, I was overwhelmed. It was exhausting. I was so tired. So, so tired of my everyday survival routine, barely catching my breath. Just so tired… and those words. Those damn words. Every time they would cross my mind – which was a few times a day since they were told to me – I flared up in anger. My body and mind were no longer the same as before. They were so tired. The anger took up so much of my energy. It tore away at me.

My sadness was a side effect of my anger. When anger consumes you, it eventually dissipates into sadness. Sadness takes the place of anger and, in time, you become bitter. At least, this was what happened with me.

Anger. Sadness. Bitterness. Fear. All my fears re-emerged.

What if it comes back? While I was in my cancer battle, I was a fearless warrior fighting to get my life back. But as I got well, fear began to re-enter my mind. Fear of reoccurrence. Fear of going bankrupt. Fear of failure. I was told by my doctors that if my aggressive cancer came back, it would likely be within the first year. If I passed the three-year mark, I'd be safe. I wondered if it came back, would I make it this time? Could I?

They say depression hits once the dust settles. That's exactly what happened.

Day became night, and night became day. Days became weeks. Two months of feeling all these paralyzing emotions. I remember walking around like a zombie. Numb.

What could I do to rid myself of all these negative emotions? Fear, regret, remorse, resentment…? The answer came to me. I had to start forgiving. Forgive for my soul to regain freedom. Let go and take back my power, and so I did. We all have demons. Some of us are not influenced by demons, but some are. Although I forgave from my heart, I knew certain people could never have a place in my life. I had to forgive without ever hearing the words, "I'm sorry." I had to forgive when I knew they had no remorse. I had to forgive them and let them go because they did not know better.

Forgiveness helped me finally snap out of it. By forgiving them and myself, I regained my power, and with that, the gift of peace within my soul. Not easy work to do, but oh so necessary for the healing process.

"They" no longer took space in my mind. That vacancy was now filled with a freedom that allowed me to function again. To think again. To feel again. I replaced my fear, my anger and sadness with love. And that's where the success lies when you start loving yourself. I came out from under the fog and said to myself, *Okay good. You felt what you needed to feel. Get up girl! Let's do this.*

So, I did – I got up and I started living with greater clarity and never went into the fog again.

With every break, I cracked open, and those cracks are what let the light back into my soul. Awakening for me came in moments captured in time. With each break, my soul healed itself from the past and opened itself to receive the lessons and the love it needed to live a life that was pure and free of the toxicity it once drowned in.

Chapter Nine

Awakening

Pay attention to your patterns. Your behavior
while surviving may not be the way you want to live.
Create new patterns to allow you to now thrive beyond survival.

– Catherine Kontos

Living Life with Purpose

Piece by piece, I built myself and my life back up, including that of my daughter's who had been broken. She rose from struggling with her school grades to becoming an Honor Roll student. From social isolation to having tons of friends. She achieved her black belt in karate and is officially a lifeguard today. The struggles she endured taught her to live a life with integrity and compassion for others. She makes me so proud. I owe my life to her. She was my only glimmer of light that kept me going when my world was dark.

My business, my social life... everything just started moving forward and up, including my love life.

Throughout those years, I went on a handful of dates and was even in a relationship for a few years. I never divulged my cancer situation immediately because I no longer saw it as what defined me. I experienced cancer. Cancer was – and is – not who I am.

As that year went on, I slowly started telling people. By the third year after, I was announcing it all over social media. The first time I posted it, I took it down almost immediately.

Eventually I gathered the courage and left the post up and continued posting different motivational or factual posts about breast cancer daily throughout breast cancer awareness month in October. It was scary to come out so publicly until the words of encouragement started to pour in. The reactions were so positive: people, including strangers, contacted me privately to say that they were going through breast cancer in secret like I had and were terrified. They would tell me how my daily posts inspired and gave them hope. They would cry and tell me how much I had helped them. Their words were priceless, and I was humbled.

To think that my coming out was helping others? I honestly thought I was just posting and perhaps even annoying people by bombarding them with daily cancer-related posts and quotes. What I found interesting was that the people who were contacting me weren't the ones pressing the "like" button on the post. It made me realize that there are a lot more people watching and being affected than I knew. This motivated me to be even more public.

On the fourth anniversary of being cancer-free, I awoke knowing, *It's time*. It was time to stop living like a survivor and start living the life of a thriver. My purpose was clear, and it was time to get going with it. I always felt that cancer patients – whether newly diagnosed, ongoing or survivors – should have a place to go, even if just for a weekend, to relax, meditate and be spoiled. I hadn't been strong enough or healed enough until now. When I needed a place to go to gather myself and make sense of my cancer diagnosis, there had been none that was exactly right. I had to book a retreat overseas, as there was nothing local to help me do so.

I started a contest, where 10 breast cancer survivors or fighters could join me at my chalet for a weekend. It was my first time out there, in so many years, helping others. It was a responsibility I took seriously. Could I do it and do it successfully? I prepared an entire program from scratch in five weeks for a weekend retreat. Within three weeks, I had been called in four times to speak live on the radio announcing this contest: the names came pouring in. Nikki even helped me make videos to post on social media, and she was pretty good at it. People were shocked when they found out a teen was filming and editing these videos.

I was passionate, committed, and obsessed with making this work. I would wake up with and go to sleep with my laptop next to me. My employees really came through for me as they took over my business. It was like someone pinned my wings so I could fly through those five weeks. I did not know how I did so much in so little time. My favorite part was calling the cancer survivors and announcing to them that they had won. The reactions from these survivors were so profound. I couldn't help but cry from happiness with them. I never expected it to have so much impact. They needed this weekend so much. My heart was overrun with pure, unadulterated joy.

Then just as the retreat weekend was approaching, I got a call that my daughter needed to go in for an endoscopy that Friday. The same Friday that all the participants would be joining me at the chalet. I begged the medical staff to move up the date, but to no avail. Nikki had been sick for eight months with her stomach and had visited the Emergency Room six times. This test was going to help finally diagnose her. There was no way I would make her wait, nor was I not going to be present during the procedure. Since I could not be at two places at the same time, I juggled everything to make it all happen. I hired someone to greet the guests as they arrived at the chalet that Friday. I brought everything up the day before so it would be ready for the next day.

As we drove back that Thursday night after dropping off the food and all the extras I needed for that weekend, I saw something unusual on the highway. It was a dead deer. It was so dark that by the time we could figure out what it was, we had driven over it, tearing the bottom of the car right off. Thank God we did not lose control. There was an 18-wheel rig driving right behind us. We pulled the car over and waited in the cold by the side of the road for help. Finally, the car was towed to a garage, and I got home safely past midnight, exhausted and questioning why there had been so many challenges that week conspiring to prevent me from going ahead. Was someone cursing this weekend retreat from happening? It was just all so strange.

The next morning, I brought Nikki to the hospital. She was sedated and had the endoscopy. I remained calm and positive that everything would turn out well, and it did. She had the procedure, and off we went to the chalet to meet everyone that evening.

The weekend was a success. There was laughter, love, and connections that developed amongst the group. We even gained a brother because breast cancer happens to men too. A bond of sisterhood with one Big Brother was formed. They were pampered and nurtured emotionally all weekend; everyone left happy. It was exactly what they needed. And I think it was exactly what I needed too because I returned home crying with joy. They did not realize the impact they had on me. By allowing me to help them, they rewarded me the gift of their time and trust. The next year, I did it again. It was incredible, once again, in a whole new different way. Again, I left overjoyed and serene.

I am blessed to have met so many beautiful souls and to be able to have provided a space for them to share their vulnerabilities, safely and without judgment. They are my heroes. They inspire me in ways that I can't describe. We all have a story, don't we? Those weekends left me with so much more than I ever expected. I had always reaped the rewards of giving, but this was beyond that. It was a peace that came along with the reward. An overwhelming feeling of gratitude that I never felt before.

They came in that weekend as survivors and graduated as thrivers, and I have not stopped flying since.

Vulnerable Love

Fall in love with their soul to never be deceived by their image.

– **Catherine Kontos**

As I was going through separation and divorce, I was sure that I would never be with another man. I felt broken, unlovable and scarred for life, literally. What man would want someone who's had cancer? I was damaged goods. My self-esteem got hit so hard. In my mind, the end of my marriage meant the end of any love life, and it was settled. I'd be single for the rest of my life, and I had to come to terms with that.

Was I ever so wrong! Although my fears of rejection made me reluctant, I gave myself permission to give dating a try. My biggest fear was having to tell them about my cancer. This is how I imagined it would go: We would start to kiss, and his hand would reach up to touch my hair. Quickly but casually, I would intercept his hand as it was about to touch my hair. I would think, *God, that was close, but what about next time? Should I go step-by-step and tell him? Oh, please don't touch my hair it's a wig.* Or should I just keep playing, intercepting? What if it became intimate? He would see my scar. For sure, I couldn't hide that. Would he reject me then? Or should I just rip off the band-aid and say, "By the way, I got myself a little cancer, and I just finished my treatments." *He would run for sure*, I thought.

All these questions. All this stress. Was dating worth it? And how soon is too soon? Was I ready? Ready or not, it happened. Cancer and all, a man was interested in me. One day, I thought I'd give him a reality check. I brought him to my oncology appointment; I even pulled off my wig at one point to scare him off because for the life of me I couldn't understand why he wanted me. My actions did not deter him. Was this compassion? I never thought that my illness would actually bring out enough compassion and sincerity for men to want to date me. But that is exactly what happened. Some women berate men as being in it for one thing, underestimating how caring a man can be. Let's not forget they are conditioned to protect and care for their women. Therefore, this type of reaction for any man with a good heart is only normal. We really need to give them more credit. In the end, we are all human and if we can't look at another person with an open heart, then we are no longer human.

> *You might be surprised how much more respect and love you will get from being genuine... flaws and all.*
>
> – **Catherine Kontos**

I had been so wrong. My perspective on dating was totally off after cancer. My thriver mindset kicked in: I went from shame and fear to pride and love. I started to wear my scar like a badge of honor that marked me not as a damaged victim, but as a warrior. It was the wound of victory.

Having gone through cancer, the idea of dating was scary because I expected to be rejected even though I knew I wouldn't want to be with a man who would do that. I couldn't risk feeling unworthy. And yet I was sure that love would find me. I was back on my feet: financially independent with an abundant social life full of supportive family, wonderful friends, and acquaintances. Most importantly, my No. 1 priority was to be the best mother I could be to my teenage daughter. So did I need a man? No, but I'm a hopeless romantic, and I wanted to find a partner to share my journey, challenges, and eventually my love. I wanted a partner who would ignite the fire to propel me forward in all my quests, and I, in turn, would be the muse to help him fulfill his dreams.

Today six years cancer-free, I am blessed to celebrate life's challenges alongside the one man who has won my heart. Meeting him changed my life in so many ways. For the first time. I met someone during a time in my life when I didn't feel broken.

One evening after a previous relationship had ended, I described to myself the type of man I wanted to find. I always went with the flow of life, knowing that our paths would eventually cross. They say, "Send out your message to the universe and the universe will bring forth to you your wishes." Well, I already knew that to be true. I had asked to get sick, and I got sick. I had asked to get well, and I got well. The mind is more powerful than we know.

Our paths crossed. He was exactly how I described him in my thoughts and in my wishes. Just like every woman, we want a man who is very passionate, affectionate, and loving. A man who is intelligent and can engage in long, intense, stimulating conversations. A man who will be a man, who steps up to protect his woman. One who understands me, my past, and loves me despite my faults. A man who respects me and has eyes only for me, who loves me with all of his heart and soul. Someone with whom I can laugh and cry without feeling guilty or judged. I had even imagined his job, ethnicity, and physicality. My man has everything I declared I wanted, almost to a T.

Throughout my journey, I always said, "I just want to be hugged." This type of hug represented more than just a hug. To me, when someone hugs you the way I needed to be hugged, it means a sense of protection against being hurt. This man holds and envelopes me with his big arms, and I feel protected. So much so, that it feels like nobody could hurt me. Along with protection, this hug represents affection and love. When someone holds you, there's a sense of peace that comes from their touch and my man did exactly that for me on our first unofficial date. We sat on a long chair. He sat behind me and I could feel his chest on my back. He held me for hours while watching the stars and listening to music. I felt so much affection and protection through this hug from a man I barely knew. It was exactly as I had envisioned it. I knew from that moment that I had found him. Exactly how I wanted him. I am safe.

He accepts me for who I am and what made me so. This can only happen for people when they accept all of who they are. How can you expect anyone to love you if you don't even love yourself? That's the question I set forth on my new path to love, and I found exactly what I wanted. I fell for the most unexpected person at the most unexpected time, at the most unexpected place. A perfect love. When you find exactly what you want, there are no more questions, just answers. Everything feels right and flows.

> *Sometimes, fear prevents us from being vulnerable to another and strips us from feeling love. I consider that punishment. Love freely and openly and reap the rewards of true happiness.*
>
> **– Catherine Kontos**

Imperfectly Perfect

After surviving cancer, there is no going back to who I was before, which is irretrievable. All that matters is who I have become after cancer. I appreciate every person, every moment and my every breath. I understand that everything and everyone is here to teach something. Every day is filled with gratitude and a deeper appreciation for all the things that before cancer went largely unnoticed: a warm breeze, a sunny porch, a good book, music, a soft touch, a loving glance, a kind word, a stranger's smile, my daughter's laughter, a bird chirping...

Through the cold and lonely winter months of treatment, I had heard the sound of a single bird chirping. It would wake me from my sleep. How magical it was to have this one bird appear outside my window in the dead of winter to soothe me with its song. I believe it was a message from my dad, that he's there watching me. It brought me comfort where there was none. I now always pay attention to the gift of a bird's song.

Now as soon as spring hits, every morning I make my coffee and sit outside in my garden terrace, soaking up the sun's rays on my face. I smell the flowers and look at their colors in what is the most peaceful moment of the day for me. I spend a good hour just absorbing nature's beauty through my eyes, through the sounds and through the soft touch of the air. I am alive. Truly alive in every sense, I feel blessed that I was given a second chance at life. My rebirth was the gift that cancer gave to me.

After my earthquake, it took years to settle the dust. I had a huge mess to clean up. Throughout that time, although my life was not quite settled because of the divorce and a struggling new business, I still felt sure that peace would come. The way I saw it, I stared down death. There was nothing I could not do. Even my nurse admitted at the end of my therapy that they had worried they would lose me during treatment. They didn't understand the gravity of my sensitivity to drugs. It was just not my time. I was a lion, strong and fierce with an inner strength and resiliency that would never allow me to be broken again. I was a lot stronger than I had given myself credit for.

I started to rebuild every part of my life, but this time on my terms.

For the first time, I know what it means to own my life, all of it – the good, the bad, the ugly. I would rebuild my life by being authentically true to myself. I would no longer bow to the expectation of others, or please anyone other than my daughter and myself.

At the age of 40, I had been spinning my wheels, going a mile a minute and scratching to-do's off my list, lost in *busy-ness* and other people's expectations. I gave in to societal pressures and conditioned expectations. I was clueless. You had to be married by a certain age and you were to have children and stay married no matter what: that "no matter what" almost killed me. I was always smiling, even if moments before I had been crying. I never showed my pain to others. I needed to fake a persona of happiness, as though I had it all together. Confident and smart, in a perfect life.

Meanwhile, living this fake persona was eating away at me every day that passed. I would wake up and go to sleep with a sense of sadness. The anxiety would wake me at night; my heart would feel heavy in the morning. My days were filled with anxiety. Not knowing how or when my life would change, I was drowning, and I didn't know how to breathe or stay afloat anymore. For years, I would have a recurring dream of being on a flooded boat, gasping for air as I fought to avoid drowning. I had lived for so many years like this. I was an unhappy soul suffering a life of misery from choices I had made. So many years wasted with negative emotions because I was too scared to live my life like I needed to in order to be happy.

Hence my experiences always seemed to falter. How could they not? How could I be happy living someone else's idea of me? At 40 years old, I still did not know who I was at the core.

I was not being fair to myself or to anyone else in my life. Throughout my life, I had counseled, owned businesses and properties, and performed voluntary services. I had made a good life for myself. By age 23, I owned my first property and was running an entire department at work. By 25, I had my own business. I suffered from depression after I had a miscarriage at 27. I decided the best thing for me to do was to go back to school to get my psychology degree – a dream I had always wanted to achieve, but could never do before due to the financial stress my family and I had lived through. I graduated with distinction and fell pregnant with Nikki. I will never diminish the good things that I did achieve at that time.

I did everything to make the best of my life or what I thought was the best. I traveled to beautiful countries, met many great people, went to dinner with friends to the best restaurants every Saturday night. I gathered with my family at my house for every holiday and enjoyed my time with them.

From the outside looking in, I had everything going for me. Meanwhile, I was breaking more and more every day. There were irreparable cracks that would eventually shatter to pieces the glass that was me. We think when we get that house or that job or that vacation, we will finally be happy. That's living in denial. I was empty inside, and I just wanted to fill that gap.

We make ourselves overwhelmingly busy, projecting the image of a fantastic life, but when none of that fills the emptiness inside, we crack. This is what happened to me the day I asked to die. God gave me my wish. He knew that what I was really begging for was to be reborn. The day I got my diagnosis was the day the *Old* Catherine died and gave way to the *New* Catherine coming alive! – reborn to live my life authentically; not caring about the disapproval of others because I chose not to live by their wishes.

> *Once you set your boundaries, the people who get upset are the ones who benefited when you had none. They will disperse from your life as this new filter you have put in place will rid you of toxic interactions, allowing only genuine relationships to blossom. That's the reward for knowing exactly who you are and where you stand in life.*
>
> **– Catherine Kontos**

Happiness is simply a pursuit, not a destination. Your destination should never be a place or a thing; it should be a different perspective and a journey filled with purpose. Seeing and experiencing life in a way that makes you happy.

Life is full of obstacles and challenges that will never change. It's a given. We have to learn to accept these challenges as life lessons. That is truly what they are. Sometimes we are bombarded by so many obstacles that we forget to live because we are so consumed by the "bad" that all we see is darkness.

What if you looked at these challenges differently? What if you didn't look at anything as being negative? I don't mean convincing yourself as such, but truly have a sense of faith about all that happens in your life. Acceptance of what is, including all your good features and all your faults. Accept yourself for who you are completely. Love every ripple of your being. You are perfectly imperfect. You are human. If you mess up, it's OK: don't be so hard on yourself. Just say to yourself that you will do better next time. That's where we should all start. Love yourself first. It's easy to say, but how does anyone do that? Where do humans start loving themselves unconditionally without fault or judgment?

Years of criticizing myself and being self-deprecating – all the way up to my 40s – hindered my growth. I denied myself experiences that could have led me to a different life. Do I regret anything? Absolutely not. I accept my journey and who I am today. I own my journey as a unique life that belongs only to me. You have to really get to know who you are and appreciate all your good and what you consider your bad. Both make up the character and person you are meant to be. Remember that we are all perfectly imperfect, and that's what makes each of us uniquely beautiful.

If you have grave challenges in life, like the death of your marriage, death of life, death of your health, or the death of your finances, know that you are not alone. Trust that even if you lose it "all" it'll be okay because when you reach rock bottom you will climb back up into who you really are meant to be, what you are truly meant to do.

The night I asked to die was my rock bottom. I went through a complete life collapse and still survived and thrived because of it. My struggle was real and long. I may not live a life based on others' approval; they may even think that I have had a bad life due to my hardships. They don't realize that all the bad I went through was the journey that allowed me to come alive. You can live 80 years wasting your life, or you can choose today to live the rest of your life your way, in happiness, whatever that happiness may be. It's there for you to choose. Be you without the worry of judgment. Be you without the worry of failure. Be you. Just be you. Choose faith over fear, and you can get through anything.

Chapter Ten

Be Brave with Your Life

Too often we dwell on the past and "what was" becomes our crutch. There's nothing we can do about the past. Let it go. It's your future that shines with your hopes and dreams. Your choices from this moment on will ignite your path to the results that you so desire.

– Catherine Kontos

Beautifully Unbreakable

Resilience is defined as, "the capacity to recover quickly from difficulties; mental toughness." Resiliency is strengthened over a lifetime. As a baby you learn to fall and get up without fear or judgment. As we go through life, the influence of our parents and surroundings gradually reprogram us to fear failure and judgment from our peers. We become entangled fighting off fears to focus on achieving our goals. At least that's our hope. To overcome our fears; not let them hinder us.

Unfortunately, it is not so black and white because life is complicated. I speak of fear when alluding to resiliency because fear is a core reason people give up. When you are getting hit from all angles, it takes courage to get up at the risk of getting hurt again and again. Why are some people able to withstand war, abuse, cancer, loss of a business, and a marriage breakdown while continuing to live well, possibly even happier than before? Yet others get hit with only one tragedy and remain bitter and depressed for the rest of their lives. It's called resiliency. How did I survive it all? How did I not remain down and shattered? How was I able to get up each time and continue?

My upbringing had a lot to do with it. By 15, I was working and helping to support myself. I paid my way through school and everything else that was needed to get by. I didn't party; I went to school and work. My Greek parents came to Canada with nothing but a suitcase and their mother tongue. I saw them work to the bone every day of the week, from morning to night, to make ends meet. They managed to own homes and build businesses; through their struggle and successes, I learned that hard work, determination, sacrifices and failures build a life, strengthening resiliency. I learned that ethic from them.

Our childhood experiences are the backbone and basis of building resiliency. That doesn't mean we can't learn it as adults. As a child, my daughter often wanted to give up on an activity that was too hard or a math problem that was just too difficult. I taught her to stop, take a break and "breathe" when she became overwhelmed by all the anxiety and frustration. She learned how other activities could distract and distance her from the stressor, allowing her to change her thoughts and feel calm. She could then contemplate the task or activity from a quieter mindset away from all the noise. She never quit anything. If at the end of the year, she no longer wanted to register for an activity the next year, that was fine: but giving up halfway through because she ran into an obstacle…never.

Oftentimes, the hits I endured were so hard that I didn't know up from down, or right from left. The noises in my head were so distracting that I could not think. How do you make life decisions when you can't even think, when your mind and soul are fearful? How do you not think, *I can't fight anymore, I give up*. Sometimes I lived by the hour because life was just too much. So we teach ourselves not to think more than we have to. If an hour ahead is all we can handle, then that's what we do. We restrict all unnecessary information and negative influences. We expel the pain from our system by crying, running, or hitting a boxing bag; whatever it takes to release the frustration, anger and sadness.

Always make sure to have a great support system and don't be afraid to ask for help from a friend who understands you and doesn't judge. There's no shame in seeking professional help. I never understood why some people feel that way. I admire those who know themselves well enough to realize that they are not perfect and seek help.

Focus on something that you know will give you strength during the hard times. For me, it was my daughter. When I needed to grasp onto something, anything, I would close my eyes and picture her face with her glistening eyes and smile. She would give me that extra push I needed to get back on the other side. It felt like lifting a 200-pound boulder over my shoulders and finding that last bit of strength to hoist it over my head. She was that for me, always.

When faced with death, the will to live is a mighty force – knowing that I am not done here and that I didn't yet fulfill my destiny can defeat even the most powerful, negative forces. I wasn't going to let anyone or anything, not even cancer, take that from me.

Find your strength when weakened muscles are all you have and let it be the wind that you need to propel you out of the darkness and into the light. YOU ARE WORTHY TO LIVE. Don't be afraid.

– **Catherine Kontos**

Another key characteristic of resiliency is recognizing and accepting it all. Think to yourself: *I can't change what happened, but I can change my reaction to it.* Have faith and find hope for a better life. Never lose sight of the light; it's what will lead you to the other side – the side you have been waiting to reach for so long. Know that you grow with every challenge; you are not breaking to break but are breaking to grow. With that perspective, there's no hit in life that will ever shatter you completely. Persevere to get back up on your feet. You are not only a survivor: you are an example to our children and the world. It's a ripple effect that will reach distances you cannot see.

I changed my perspective on all the so-called "bad" things that happened to me. I considered them all a gift, including cancer. Cancer returned to me the life I was meant to live. It almost killed me before I came alive. Many others' lives are stripped with no last goodbye, but God gave me a chance to fight. Before cancer, I was questioning living. I got my answer with my diagnosis. I was given the option to die. It was like He was telling me, "Do you really want to die? I just gave you the key to open death's door. Your choice: choose to die or choose to live."

Not only did I not want to die: I chose to come alive with purpose and gratitude. So when people look at my swollen right arm (due to the removal of my lymph nodes) and commiserate, I say to them: "If this was the price I had to pay to make me come into the fullness of my life, then it was a small price to pay."

Feeling like a victim brings bitterness to your heart. Life's challenges become increasingly weighty as they pile one on another, conspiring to break you. Try changing your perspective and looking at your challenges as teachings and blessings. Each challenge is a step forward, not a step backward, even if it feels that way. When the next challenge comes – as bad as it might seem, or as dark as it might get, – you will not perceive the previous challenges as weight holding you down. You will find your way through, knowing they will pass just like the others did in the past, and life will reward you, putting you a step closer to where you want to be.

Be kind to yourself. Learn how to recover your body and mind. Exercise and release all the "happy chemicals" in your brain. Meditate and breathe calmly; eat nutritious foods and avoid those that cause you to feel tired or anxious. Do a lot of what you love because self-love is a huge component in giving you the strength to fight. Do whatever you need to do to sleep well. Sleep regenerates the mind and the body. Lack of sleep will hurt you. It will cause you to feel sad, anxious, with a very low tolerance to cope with stress. Sleep is absolutely crucial to recovery and sustaining a resilient mindset.

The hardest component of resiliency – which is an integral part of love and often neglected – is forgiveness of yourself and others. How better to love yourself? Stop being so harsh on yourself.

Understand that others are not living the same journey as you, and they do so with their own perspective. Forgive them. Anger and resentment will keep you down. Remove negativity: let it and them go. Free yourself to fly out of the cage that has confined you for so long.

Becoming resilient is a practice. It does not happen overnight. It is truly mind over matter. Resiliency is built by foregoing fear, accepting your situation, and being optimistic with an undeterred focus, lots of self-love, faith, and hope.

It consists of training your mind to look at the stressors positively. See how they can help you versus hurt you. Stay hopeful. Don't be afraid or embarrassed to ask for help and support. Keep your friends close. Focus on a goal and something or someone that gives you strength. Love yourself, unconditionally. Your strengths, your faults, everything. You are unique. Your faults give you character.

Everything is surmountable. You just need the vision to see on the other side of that hill.

Embracing My Reality

> *Change perspective and see how life brightens.*
>
> – **Catherine Kontos**

Whatever the trauma – be it psychological, physical, or caused by disease – it does not always go away with treatment. Unfortunately, trauma can continue even after the initial battle is won. Those who have never experienced grave trauma do not realize this. They think that when treatment is over that the battle has been won. People will throw parties to celebrate the end of treatment, and that's great because ending treatment should be celebrated. But many continue to suffer behind closed doors. The trauma happened and continues to happen to you after it's long gone. It's the challenge after the challenge.

The biggest obstacle is the fear that resides within every survivor. I believe survivors suffer a form of post-traumatic stress disorder. When someone has their life seriously threatened, it shakes them upside down. This is trauma. And when "the cure" comes and it's all over, it's not really "all over". Death becomes your reality and you can no longer live in denial. You start fighting for your life. When you get the initial shock of a life-threatening diagnosis, you switch to fight mode, usually and hopefully with much support. When the treatments stop, people often think you're fine. What they don't realize is that cancer scars you with both after-effects and side effects. Depending on your mental state, your perspective will either gravitate towards fear and sadness or towards acceptance, whereby you restructure the goals of your new life.

The cancer survivor may look fine, but they are often left scared, in pain, and with countless medical appointments. Financially, they are drained and are always trying to balance work with their appointments. Many are also left with broken relationships and find themselves being single parents. Being insecure about their diagnosis and body image, they have a hard time getting back into the dating scene. The single thing that every cancer survivor most fears is a recurrence. No matter how well you're coping, you know that this is a possibility because it was once your reality.

This book speaks a lot about cancer, but it could be about anything that depletes and deprives you of the joy that life can bring. An abusive marriage, an illness of any kind, a situation where you feel only darkness – all these are challenges and obstacles. You can give up and let them eat away at you, or you can accept them and make a decision not to suffer. Pain is inevitable: we will all get hurt at one point, but suffering is a choice.

I chose not to suffer any longer mentally, emotionally or physically so I took it in my hands to reshape my life, not only as I went through the worst of times, but every single day since. Mental toughness is a muscle, and we can all build it up.

The hardest and most important lesson of my life came when I was diagnosed: there is no such thing as control. I used to think I could control my destiny, but control is a lie we tell ourselves. Knowing that one day my life could change the way it did six years ago motivates me to live life to its fullest. I no longer think long term. I'm on a five-year renewal. If it feels good, if it feels right and nobody is getting hurt, then go for it. Why wait for tomorrow? I have taken so much time out of my life worrying about the future. Tomorrow may not come. From the minute we are born, with every day that passes, we are one day closer to death. That's the truth whether you like to hear it or not. To me, this is not negative. It is quite a positive way to live. I live for today. I appreciate my today. I am grateful for today and will always be grateful for the gift of tomorrow.

Reality hit hard when I understood that the only thing I could control was how I handled myself when faced with the circumstances of my life. I am not saying not to act in preventative ways. What I am saying is to do what you feel you need to do in life to live your best; don't act in ways that allow fear to become your driving force. If it's all that propels you, fear will destroy you. Do whatever it takes to get past the fear, and you will find slivers of light and love moving in to replace it. This shift in perspective will change your entire being. This is where awakening shines its light, and you come alive.

Smile. Love your body. Love yourself. Be kind. Be gracious. Be generous. Most of all, have faith that all will be as it should. Everything that happens, as small as it may be, affects the circle of life, even if you don't see it. Trust in your journey, Cease trying to control, and just live.

My collapse was so overall consuming that I expected it to take about five years to get back on my feet. My life post-cancer has not been easy, and yet I'm happier than I've ever been. Through the worst of times, I managed to clean up a government tax audit, I endured an emotionally and financially draining divorce, and I watched my business crumble before turning things around by launching a new one. Hey I stared death in the face and I'm still here!

My biggest challenge has been the chalet. It needed a lot of TLC, and I had to deal with construction companies, engineers, and city officials on my own in order to fix it up.

I dreaded the call from my caretaker that the retaining wall had fallen or the foundation needed repair; the burden of financing and responsibility was all on me. At one point, I was days away from having to ask a friend for a personal loan. I had to sell the building I had bought for my parents to pay for it all.

I remember when I bought that building, I knew my father's heart was very weak. He was one wrong heartbeat away from death. My dream was to give back to him what he had once lost. A home. When I moved my parents to their new home, I asked God to give him at least six months to enjoy it. He was so happy. He painted and built a wooden gazebo on his deck and was making plans to plant a great big garden in the back yard. He was so proud to call it his home. God granted me my wish. He did get to enjoy it for six months. Eight years later, I had no choice but to sell it. This broke my heart.

She (the chalet) came to me a little broken and messy, just when I was also messed up and broken – she was my baby. I breathed love into her and she came alive. And even though she may still have some small wounds to mend, she has blossomed into the soul-filled building she is now. We have both flourished with an inpouring of love throughout the years. The chalet has even shown me its appreciation. One day my neighbor came to visit. I showed him the new 40-foot retaining wall I had just built. He looked and noticed on the wall an image made of moss that was shaped as two hearts. I said to him with a smile and joy in my heart, "That's her thanking me."

This chalet and I are beautifully broken, and our scars are a symbol of rebirth. My long shiny hair used to be a big part of how I identified myself, but now it's the scars that I embrace and identify with. It took being cut open by an oncology surgeon to remove all the bad that was festering within, so I could live the life meant for me. Today I wear my scar with pride.

AFTERWORD - Stop Surviving. Start Thriving.

There is always something to be grateful for; never forget that the slightest spark can grow into a raging fire, and we all have a spark inside. Light yours into a beast of a fire that will strengthen you day by day.

Remember that we only get this one life; there are no do-overs; so don't waste a minute with anything or anyone that bring you down. Those are minutes you never get back. Cherish every second you have with your loved ones. You never know when life will twist the story. You can feel amazing, and in one second, your life changes forever. So when life is good, take that time and fly like a bird in life's beautiful moments. Breathe it all in because when life challenges you, that's when the fires rage with the belief that you will rise stronger, better and more aligned with your true self than ever before.

There is a Greek song named *O Aetos*, which translates into *The Eagle*. It's a song that has so much meaning, reminding me of my dad. Every time I listen or dance to it, I fall into a trance feeling every word. One of the more meaningful lyrics that touch my soul is as follows:

And if you burn my wings
not to fly again
from my fire's smoke
again I will fly high
the eagle dies in the air
free and strong

(Και αν μου κάψεις τα φτερά
να μην ξαναπετάξω
απ᾽της φωτιάς μου τον καπνό
πάλι ψηλά θα φτάσω.
Ο αετός πεθαίνει στον αέρα
ελεύθερος και δυνατός)

That's exactly how I felt throughout my journey. Like a bird with clipped and burnt wings, yet I still flew and rose above, the smoke propelling me higher and further than ever before. I forgive every person and even cancer for trying to burn my wings. In fact, I thank them for igniting the smoke that propelled me to reach heights I only imagined.

You changed my life, and I am grateful for the abundance I live every day.

> *Never allow anyone to limit your capabilities. Smash those limitations and watch the doubters rub their eyes in disbelief. Remember that YOU are one of a kind.*
>
> **– Catherine Kontos**

"Whirlwind" by Catherine Kontos 2014

A self-portrait of a time where everything was unraveling. Stripped bare naked, vulnerable to all that surrounded her and protecting herself from all the chaos.

A woman with a fierce undeterred vision for a bright future.

Biography

Catherine Kontos, Resiliency Coach, BA(psy), DipM

Catherine Kontos, a multi-scholar award winner, holds a bachelor's degree with distinction in psychology and a diploma in marketing. She has won multiple awards in recognition of her business and personal achievements. She has been featured in magazine, newspaper, and radio news coverage.

Trained in mindfulness-based stress reduction (MBSR), she is a multifaceted professional, using her skills in counseling, business, marketing, real estate, and design in both her investment and coaching businesses. During both her career as a volunteer and a counselor in hospitals, health centers and private practice, Catherine has worked with patients suffering from addictions, disorders and illnesses, including Alzheimer's, depression, and anxiety. She teaches empowerment to her clients through speaking engagements, private sessions, group sessions, and retreats – both in-person and online.

Her priority is her work as a philanthropist. Although Catherine has always dedicated her time as a volunteer to many different institutions, causes, and committees, her true purpose was ignited when she was diagnosed with breast cancer in 2013. Since then she has hosted, assisted, and has spoken in multiple charity events. She is also the founder of SunHill Retreats which hosts The Pink Mountain Retreat weekend for breast cancer survivors.

Her mission since she was diagnosed with breast cancer has been to use her voice to help as many people as she can who are suffering from this horrible disease. Her approach in all that she does, both personally and professionally, is to inspire others by guiding them – through her experience and knowledge – on how to survive any challenge life brings. She uses those challenges to induce in her clients a state of mind that will help them thrive and find their life's purpose. Her first retreat came to life in the fall of 2017 on the fourth anniversary of her being cancer-free.

This was her way of giving back, fulfilling her promise to help others. It was a very spontaneous decision (five weeks planning), funded mostly from her savings and with the help of some volunteers and the generosity of some restaurants and grocers who provided food. Her 77-year-old mom and 14-year-old daughter were by her side, helping make the entire weekend a great success.

Hand-in-hand, three generations have brought these empowering retreats to life. The survivors who come in as survivors and graduate as thrivers are spoiled with gifts and spend a free weekend in the mountains. They can enjoy massages, reiki and life-empowering sessions of yoga, tai chi and meditation – all while eating delicious, nutritious food prepared by a private chef.

During the weekend retreats, there is an indescribable bond that emerges. By the simple act of sharing and being with each other, the survivors break through the challenges and struggles of their cancer and life after cancer. The sense of lone wolf disappears and a lifetime of sisterhood – and sometimes brotherhood – is built. They leave with a different outlook and excitement about conquering life. They leave knowing they will always have a shadow.

"It was humbling and empowering. A once-in-a-lifetime, mind-opening, life-altering weekend. Catherine brought together 10 survivors – 10 strangers – who had an instant connection without even saying a word. It was the first time I felt surrounded by people who understood what I had been through... because they had been through it too. It was a true gift."

– Adina Moss – thriver 2017

Photo credit: Adina Moss for SunHill Retreats

"I attended the Pink Mountain Retreat in November 2018. During this weekend, our minds, spirits, bodies, and souls were nourished beyond belief. I felt inspired by Cat and the nine other breast cancer survivors who attended the retreat. These women have become my friends. I felt a sense of empowerment in taking back my life after breast cancer. I am proud to say I am not only a survivor but a thriver as well."

– Allison Friedman – thriver 2018

Photo credit: Nikki for SunHill Retreats

"It was a wonderful experience to share with all the amazing thrivers…ladies and a special gentleman. What made it even more special was having my sister there as well. She and I shared tears with her diagnosis, then two years later, she helped me wipe my tears with my diagnosis. Special memories that I will always carry in my heart."

– Voula Andrianopoulos – thriver 2017

A portion of the funds obtained from sales of this book will be contributed to these weekend retreats and cancer charities.

My goal is to help you re-center your mind, body, and spirit and to let go of thoughts and behaviors that prevent you from living optimally so that a renewed and fulfilled self can emerge. I am a resiliency coach. I am a life-empowering coach. I help my clients break their barriers and teach them to cope with life's challenges by changing their perspective to a more positive one. Where one must take these obstacles and learn to thrive from them, learn to become resilient and come alive to a more gratifying life.

– Catherine Kontos

ACKNOWLEDGMENTS

First and foremost, I'd like to thank the fiercest fighter I know, my daughter, Nikki, who went through all of this with me at the age of 10 and is now a thriving young woman.

Thank you for being my angel of light during our darkest time. I may have given you life, but you gave me strength to fight for my life back.

I wrote most of this book watching the beautiful ocean in Cuba. I would not have been able to write about my difficult journey and relive the emotions without having my special someone wipe away my tears. Henry, you were my breath when I could not breathe and the hug I so yearned for throughout this journey. Thank you for loving me through the tears, pain, and joys of writing this book.

My mother, who has always been by my side, supporting me mentally and physically when I was too weak even to get out of bed. My special "fight partners", especially Vicky who stepped in and brought me to many of my chemotherapy treatments and Toni for holding me up when my knees felt like buckling.

Thank you to my family and friends who were the wind that helped me fly with clipped wings, especially my siblings Frank, Lisa, Bessie; my cousins Popi and Frank, as well as the ones already mentioned in this book.

All who sponsored and supported The Pink Mountain Retreat for breast cancer survivors, especially my good friends Lilla, Mariana, Grace and the late Sammy.

All the beautiful survivors who joined me at the retreats. You are my heroes.

Thank you to all my doctors and nurses at the Royal Victoria Hospital; especially Dr. Thirwell and nurse Kathy; Dr. Brabant,

my surgeon at St. Mary's Hospital; Dr. Hope, my general practitioner; as well as the Wellness Center at the MUHC in Montreal. You helped me cope with all the unpredictable twists and turns of my journey.

The MUHC Foundation for always supporting me and raising awareness and funds for breast cancer along with their many partners, such as Pink in the City, and Donnabella; all which I support and, in return, have supported me and many others.

RESOURCES (visit: www.catherinekontos.com)

REFERENCES: Notis Sfakianakis. "O Aetos." *Notioanatolika Tou Kosmou,* lyricstranslate.com.

Made in the
USA
Monee, IL

14781245R00095